Telephone: MOUntview 3343.

HIGHGATE LITERARY & SCIENTIFIC INSTITUTION

11, SOUTH GROVE, N.6.

9555

Time allowed FOURTEEN Days

Date Issued	Date Issued	Date Issued
6 DEC 1957		
17 DEC 1957		
23 JAN 1958		
5 JUL 1984		

3000-3-54

NO IDLE WORDS

Some books by the same author

MASTER SANGUINE
A Satire

I COMMIT TO THE FLAMES
A Survey

MARINE PARADE
A Novel

PARTIES OF THE PLAY *and* FIRST PLAYER
Histories of Theatre

BROWN STUDIES
Essays

AMAZING MONUMENT (with George Fearon)
The Story of the Shakespeare Industry

IVOR BROWN'S BOOK OF WORDS
I GIVE YOU MY WORD
SAY THE WORD
Anthologies of Words

NO IDLE WORDS

by

IVOR BROWN

JONATHAN CAPE
THIRTY BEDFORD SQUARE
LONDON

FIRST PUBLISHED 1948

Dewey Classification
422

PRINTED IN GREAT BRITAIN IN THE CITY OF OXFORD
AT THE ALDEN PRESS
BOUND BY A. W. BAIN & CO. LTD., LONDON

INTRODUCTION

My reasons for offering the public a fifth in this series of Word Books are the same as those which prompted my earlier successors to *A Word in Your Ear*. The writing of them needs no continuous application and can therefore be fitted into the corners of a fairly busy journalistic life. They have been recommended by my kindly critics as Bed Books. The phrase has in this case a double application: for some part, at least, of the books has been manufactured in bed. By noting a striking word or passage in one's midnight reading some material was made ready for comment during Sunday's leisure. Sabbath-breaking has been a frequent condition of getting on with a job that was light and, to me at least, agreeable.

But what I found for myself in this way was only a portion. Once more I have been most generously fed, even at times most vigorously prodded, by word-fanciers. To them I again express my deepest gratitude for the way in which they do my work for me. To find paper, to take up pen, to write, stamp, and dispatch letters is a form of manual labour from which I habitually shrink. But the world is full of hardier and more energetic folk to whom the sight of a writing-pad is no deterrent. Hours of work have gone to providing me with information and suggestions. I attach a list of the principal authors of this book; they remain financially unrewarded as before, but this does not deflect the stream of co-operation. We hear much of 'incentives' in these days. They mean nothing to my counsellors. Among them the amateur spirit is unquenchable, with much benefit to the unworthy professional, myself.

My efforts to amend the public and official use of English are naturally unavailing. Where Sir Alan Herbert is signally defeated, I need not be ashamed of my place in the rout. By Sir Ernest Gowers, Sir Wilfrid Eady and others our bureaucrats are being commanded to drop their Barnacular and write like human beings. But few signs of reform appear. The educators remain as bad as the administrators. Our statesmen continue to say 'I am at a loss to understand' when they mean 'I cannot understand'. I observe that teaching children is now called 'the liquidation of illiteracy'.

Have there been any ups and downs in the verbal vogues since my last volume? Evocative has moved up several places in the English of the literary gentlemen and will soon be elbowing integrated for supremacy in what may be called 'criticese', which is the jargon of the more august 'pudderers'. It is a stupid adjective unless further defined – and then it becomes clumsy. Plainly a work of art must evoke something, if only tedium. To say that it evokes without saying what it evokes is to say nothing whatever. Still, saying nothing whatever has always been a respected part of the higher criticism. Evocative is long and pompous and helps the critic out in his awkward moment, i.e. when he has to fill his space and has no idea what to say. I have been in that plight myself: escape would have been so much easier if evocative had been the fashion then. 'The finely integrated elements of this evocative and satisfying book.' No doubt, that is the way to look like saying something!

The absurd use of over-all is still expanding. You rarely see the shorter words whole and total in journalism nowadays. Output is never total, but always over-all. 'Janus' in the *Spectator*, shrewd in judgment and sharp of phrase, has given over-all his well-merited malison: but it is impossible to dislodge a vogue word within a few years. Time alone may wear it down. So we shall continue to read about 'the over-all intake of fillers in the lower income groups' when facts about poor peoples' food are being compiled.

The films have taken up schizophrenic with rare gusto: the picture-makers either cannot or will not let it rest. Even in would-be popular columns where 'crackers', 'loopy', and 'bats' used to suffice, schizophrenic now rears its monstrous head. The unfortunate film-goers, lacking Greek, make efforts to cope with it and sometimes come embarrassingly out of the struggle. But no doubt it justifies the pride of a science-hungry nation to use so earned a term. We are undoubtedly, as was said, 'liquidating illliteracy'.

Now for my list of obligations.

I am indebted to Miss Allen and Miss Catt for secretarial help. The following list of stimulators, question-raisers, and co-authors may not be complete, since letters will pursue one on holiday and so fail to get answered or filed. To those overlooked, my apologies: to all, whether mentioned or not, my gratitude.

IVOR BROWN

February 1948

Mrs. H. M. Addison
Norah Airey
Janet Ashbee
Catherine Avent

S. S. Barnaby
Vernon Bartlett
C. V. Bliss
R. Bloxham
C. L. Boltz
Stephen Bone
Miss M. Brady
C. Neville Brand
Leonard Brockington
W. J. Brown
Frank Buckland
Margaret Bullivant

Denis Caseley
Miss A. M. Clark
Sir George T. Clerk
F. D. Crowther

Margaret Denny
A. E. Dingle
Thomas Dunbabin

F. Edmonson
L. E. Eyles

Daniel George
S. Godman
W. L. Goodman

Mrs. A. Hall
Otto Heinertz
May Elliott Hobbs
Dr. W. B. Howell
E. A. C. Husbands

W. Jesper

C. A. Keeble

Diamid Kelly
C. Kent-Wright

W. S. MacCunn
J. McEccles
Moray MacLaren
Mrs. A. E. MacLeod
Michael H. Marshall

Iain Orr
Harrison Owen

Sir James Peck
Stewart Perowne
A. L. Plairré

Anthony Reiss
V. Richard
George Richards
C. B. Ricks
W. H. D. Rouse

Gillian Sale
T. H. Savory
A. B. Stewart
Ruth Stuart

J. C. Trewin

Mrs. C. L. Visser

H. T. Walls
Viscount Wavell
Dorothy Weymouth
Dr. Thomas Wood
J. H. Wright
R. V. Wright

ALIEN

ALIENS now are matter for legislation, ordinance, and restriction. The word has unhappy and unpleasant associations. We think of ourselves as Britons abroad, never as aliens. A dull word? Surely its adjective has immense potentialities of pathos. It rings with melancholy like a sea-bird's plaint above the waters. We all know of Ruth's sad heart,

When sick for home,
She stood in tears amid the alien corn.

Sick for home! How much better than the ubiquitous 'nostalgic' of our day, the nostalgic without which no critical column can now be written. There is a short poem by Alice Meynell called 'Rivers Unknown to Song' which begins,

Wide waters in the waste: or, out of reach,
Rough Alpine falls, where late a glacier hung;
Or rivers, groping for the alien beach,
Through continents, unsung.

That is exquisite and its poignant picturing of wilderness is well assisted by the use of alien. 'Groping for the alien beach' is a fine phrase for the first stirrings of a great river in the hills and for the early meanderings of a mountain beck.

A long 'a' not only occurs in separation, but powerfully suggests the pains of parting. I have continually echoing in my mind various lines about this theme of alienation in all of which the same letter occurs and sets the tune. 'Over the hills and faraway', described by G. K. Chesterton as one of the most beautiful lines in all English poetry, gains vastly by the long 'a' at the close. Then there are the often quoted and unforgettable lines of uncertain origin,

From the lone shieling of the misty island
Mountains divide us and a waste of seas;
Yet still the blood is strong, the heart is Highland,
And we in dreams behold the Hebrides.

That last line derives great advantage from the roll of 'Hebrides' and the alternating alliterations. The 'br' so aptly follows the 'dr' in dreams and the 'h' effectively echoes those in heart and Highland. But the note of exile is first sounded in 'a waste of seas'. The long 'a', following a series of 'i's, has curious power; 'a waste of seas' seems to stretch out for ever. Did not the title of Eliot's 'Waste Land' profit greatly by that long 'a' and give just the right effect? Then, another echo tossing in the waste of waters in my memory, is Matthew Arnold's

The unplumb'd, salt, estranging sea.

Strange is such a common word that we do not pause to notice the spell inherent in this long-drawn monosyllable. It is surely worth remark that Keats, when using the word alien with such skill, followed it with a row of 'a's, including 'magic casements', and 'faery lands'. The letter does its work again in farewell. Shakespeare's infallible instinct for sending pain sounding through our hearts made him describe departure with a peal of 'a's.

Farewell! A long farewell to all my greatness
This is the State of Man.

The 's's at the beginning of the second line are awkward, but the repeated vowel sounds a last post with strong appeal to our compassion.

AMBER

AMBER always stirs and slightly satisfies romantic cravings. The worst writing is full of it. *Forever Amber* was a novel which lived on its name as well as on its sins. I was deflected from reading it by the nature of the publicity it received, but I am told that, if you could endure the monotony of its amorous goings-on, it gave a lively and intelligent picture of the Restoration scene, at least for the reader who was not a profound historical student or a specialist in the seventeenth century. The immense public favour shown to it was much assisted, I am sure, by the romantic mellifluity of the title.

Amber is handsome stuff and its name fits into melody so happily that writers of all qualities often start to play with it. Oscar Wilde, who could, when he preferred it, write as badly as any, turned out some effectively vulgar tosh in his *Salome* and Herod's speech therein about the resources of his regalia piles jewel on jewel until one begins to laugh at so much lapidary parade. Dickens has been rebuked for mixing his prose with blank verse when he was 'wibrating' our heart-strings, as Tappertit would have said: but what of Wilde's metrical spasms in his more berylled and chrysoprastic passages? Says Herod, 'In a coffer incrusted with amber I have sandals incrusted with glass'. Damnably uncomfortable, one would think. But the crustation of the royal shoe-cupboard with amber sets the romantic note. That sort of writing invites to the capping of lines. 'In a coffer incrusted with amber, I have sandals incrusted with glass; and I play on my viol de gamba and charm all the snakes in the grass.' Wilde also dealt out carbuncle and jade, onyxes and topazes; but onyxes and topazes are ugly and gawky sounds, especially in the plural. The jewel-merchants of letters, are, however, for ever safe with amber. I do not believe that Herrick's Julia had musical instruments made of that material, but the Parson could not resist the roll of the word.

> So smooth, so sweet, so silv'ry, is thy voice
> As, could they hear, the damn'd would make no noise,
> But listen to thee, walking in thy chamber,
> Melting melodious words to lutes of amber.

There is the very soul of ambergris-poesy in that last line. Lutes by the way, as well as amber, were always popular with the *fin de siècle* poets of the eighteen-nineties.

> For gardens where I know not if I find
> Autumn or spring about the shadowy fruit,
> And if it is the sighing of the wind
> Or if it is the sighing of the lute.

This from *Faint Love* by Arthur Symons, written for a fan. (I mean a fan not a 'fan'.) Surely it should have been a lute made of amber. Will that sort of poetry come again? There should be room for all sorts, including the sadly-sweet, with its soft lutes of love and tresses of amber hue.

AMULET

THE mythical schoolboy who defined an amulet as a Danish omelette may have been wrong, but, since Danish omelettes are made with fresh and plentiful eggs, they have their proper magic. Amulets, worn to defy witches, murrains, and evil sprites, have an oriental sound; if you want to be more classical you call them periapts as did La Pucelle in the (probably Shakespearean) First Part of *Henry VI.*

Now help, ye charming spells and periapts

cried this unsaintly Joan, who was made to rely upon conjuror's arts as well as on the 'choice spirits that admonish me', i.e. the Voices of her holy guardians and attenders. The dealers in amulets and periapts may be called necromancers and there again we run into a strange word. Necromancy ought to mean prophecy by corpse, for the Greek mantis was a prophet and necron was a dead body; we keep the latter term in necropolis for cemetery. But the necro in necromancy is a confusion, apparently, with the Latin *niger*, black: hence the word means prophecy by black art or black magic. Here is certainly a barbarous marriage of two languages and the child which it produces is dusky. Periapt is at least a true Grecian. But it sounds like a piece of architecture, whereas amulet does sound like a piece of magic.

AMYGDALINE

SHOULD our poets ever return to the Tennysonian iambic I recommend this adjective to their attention. It means almond-like, for almond appears to be derived from the Greek amygdal. The almond tree has made great music in its time. When 'fears shall be in the way and the almond-tree shall flourish and the grasshopper shall be a burden and desire shall fail: because man goeth to his long home and the mourners go about the streets'. The amygdaline blossom, coming, as it does, when the east wind may still be snell, is a great heartener of mankind and I do not know why the Preacher linked the almond with mourning and with lamentation. But one thing is certain; amygdaline would handsomely end a ten-syllable verse about the colour-scheme of March or early April. Perhaps, too, the word would fitly decorate one of those ladies who must have their hair in the hue of a blanched almond. Amygdaline blondes are many and the epithet would give them more dignity than they usually possess.

There is one odd thing about the amygdal or almond. Amygdalitis means inflammation of the tonsils; presumably the disease is deemed to give these potential nuisances the size of almonds; but it scarcely bestows upon them the pleasing quality of the word, the smooth amygdaline benignity.

ANIMADVERT

NOTICING in the preface to a book that its author called a misprint a 'Typographical inadvertence', thus lavishly giving his readers nine syllables for two, I was reminded of those fillers of the correspondence columns who insist upon animadverting on their pet themes or grievances. The verb is a simple Latinism for turning the mind towards, but seemingly one cannot thus turn the mind without the spur of rage. For animadversion now seems always to imply censure. The noun is long and cumbrous, but somehow appeats less odd and foolish than the verb. 'Do you animadvert on me, Sir?' is not common conversational English, but indignant letter-writers in the Press do frequently allude to those who animadvert on this cause or that person.

Surely the word animadvertisement should also exist. Perhaps the bureaucrats will develop its use. After all, what craft-proud Civil Servant would willingly use four monosyllables in a row

('You Have Been Warned')? It would be so much more impressive to translate this into officialese. 'A public animadvertisement concerning the dangers inherent in . . .' Do we like this kind of thing? No. I, for my part, animadvert thereon. So do I also animadvert on blaming typographical inadvertence when you have failed to read your proofs. I am a shamefully bad proof-reader myself, because I get so bored and embarrassed with reading what I have written. But, when slips pass in the night, they shall be slips with me or plain mistakes, certainly not inadvertences.

APOGEE

WE turn to Greek and Arabic (apogee and zenith on the one hand and nadir on the other) to signify triumph and disaster. In each case we fetch our metaphor from the heavens. Apogee means 'from the earth' in Greek and a crossword craftsman could doubtless weave some ingenuity about a Greek getting to heaven by falling off an English horse. Our apogee, 'the meridional altitude of the sun on the longest day' is more often used in a metaphorical than in an astronomical sense and signifies the summit of success. Apogee, mixing mid-summer with glory, should go with roses, 'those blood-drops from the burning heart of June', as well with laurels and bays, the symbols of acclamation.

There is an adjective apogean, which, one feels, ought to be in Swinburne and possibly is. Had there been film-stars in his younger days, had Hollywood and Denham then rivalled the Italian cities and the isles of Greece as a source of hymns to beauty, he might surely have dealt in the apogee of what is now so curtly known as S.A., Oomph, and It. May I suggest the following as possible A.C.S.?

The sovereign of stars we install you
  On the zenith of fame, or beyond;
The human tornado we call you,
  The love-bitten blonde.

We bring to you worship and paean,
  You have gold in your voice (and your bank);
On your brows are the bays apogean,
  Fair Lady of Rank.

As we list to the sound-track with glad ear,
  We vow that yours ever shall be,
Instead of decline to the nadir,
  Prolonged apogee.

The opposite of apogee is nadir, usually meaning the point in the heavens diametrically opposite to the zenith, which was an Arabian form of apogee. Nadir has established itself firmly in the cliché country by now and, as a journalist who is sick of the sight of it, I should avoid nadirs in a leading article. But it has been esteemed in its time and to be in the vocabulary of A. E. Housman is an honour indeed.

See, in mid-heaven the sun is mounted: hark
The belfries tingle to the noonday chime,
'Tis silent, and the subterranean dark
Has crossed the nadir and begins to climb.

What a choice of verb is tingle for the bell-resonant tower! Had the text been an old one some fussy editor would have emended it to tinkle.

APOZEME

THE language of the old medicos as well as of the Alchemists is a rich pasture. Their favourite potions were Ptisanes – a lofty title for barley-water – or Electuaries, which were syrups containing medicinal powders. I like also the decoction called an Apozeme. Shakespeare's son-in-law, Dr. Hall, specialized in the treatment of scurvy, then a common complaint owing to the lack of vegetables after winter had arrived and also to the monotonous diet of salted meat. Many of the patients whom he described were scorbutic. One feels very sorry for his Lady Underhill who suffered, as the vulgar say now, from 'ants in the pants' or at least from a similar type of itch. However, Hall soon had the nuisance in hand.

> The Lady Underhill, aged 53, was troubled with pain of the joynts in the hands and when she rubbed one with another there arose a flatulous tumor, she had also a sudden red face – her voyce was also much lost so that when she spoke the bystanders could not understand her, she felt as it were biting of ants in many parts of her body and these from scurvy . . . [the treatment follows] . . . and she became very well and so highly praised the apozeme as if it wrought by enchantment.

Upward and onward, her ladyship may well have said, with the ptisanes, the electuaries, and, not least, the apozemes! Might we not all place immediate confidence in a doctor who left us a prescription with so lofty a title?

BALDERDASH

WHEN that great figure of farce, Mr. Robertson Hare, chin up, skull and spectacles aglitter, and all the bourgeois virtues and indignations steaming from his outraged dignity, cries 'Balderdash', the audience is always in a roar. But how many know what balderdash is, except a synonym for nonsense? One (too learned) schoolboy defined it as a poem by Matthew Arnold. (He was only three letters out.) It is a verb as well as a noun. Balderdashing is, in fact, mixing your drinks. Balderdash began as beer and butter-milk mingled, which sounds sufficiently odious, and then was applied to beer and wine or to any alcoholic jumble. In this sense the punches and the cocktails are all balderdash. But they are mixed for strength, while the old balderdash seems to have been assembled for weakness, as in the case of shandy-gaff, and so came to signify feeble, confused ideas. The dictionaries are unhelpful about shandy-gaff (beer and ginger-beer or lemonade mixed). This is a popular summer drink and vastly improved, in the opinion of some, by being further balderdashed with a spot of gin.

Balderdash was a verb in the eighteenth century. Smollett railed at some of the stuff sold as wine in his day: 'A vile, unpalatable, and pernicious sophistication, balderdashed with cider, corn-spirit, and the juice of sloes.' Why do we always assume that those were the 'good old days' for the consumer? Any reader of eighteenth-century travels realizes that inn-keeping Boniface, as generous as rubicund, with a conscience as spotless as his apron, is a romantic dream of our own time. The inns were mainly as dirty and bad as the roads, much of the food tough and filthy, and the drinks balderdash. In the great Palladian houses of the nabobs, in Brighton or in Berkeley Square, larder and cellar may have been admirable, but the ordinary visitor in town or village stood every chance of a verminous couch and of a poor medley of liquor and victuals.

BAMBOOZLE

To bam was an eighteenth-century term for 'to cozen' or 'deceive by treachery'. But it was beaten in popularity by cog: that is, as far as the brief terms were concerned. One reads of cogging, not of bamming, politicians. Bam has lived on in its longer form, bamboozle. Swift describes bamboozle as one of a series of words 'invented by some pretty Fellows and now struggling for the Vogue'. Bamboozle did not struggle in vain, but it has lost class. It is now hardly to be described as in the vogue. You would not expect to see it in a leader in *The Times*. 'The Government have bamboozled the electorate.' No, I think this would hardly do in Printing House Square, however tempting and expressive the term may be.

Can there be innocent bamboozling? Can it mean unpurposed misleading rather than guileful deceit? I have heard this claimed by a writer whose usage of bamboozle I challenged. I said that he might be involved in a libel action by his application of bamboozle to a certain important person's behaviour, because the word implied dishonesty, deliberate fraud, and mischievous intention. The writer replied that bamboozle only meant confuse and that a politician might confuse the public or the Cabinet in his well-meant and quite honest stupidity. So no charge of libel could be brought. But I could not agree. Nor do the dictionaries. Bamboozling has been generally regarded as a form of dirty work, not of clean folly; and a very satisfactory word, in that connection, it most certainly is.

BARRICADE

SUCH a word is indeed an asset to rebellion. First it was a defence-work made of barrels. Then it came to mean a street-rampart made of any useful and available objects, such as wagons, furniture, and whatever might be handy for those holding a seized position in a street or public place during a civic revolt. Barricades, accordingly, are part of the music of insurrection. There is a sonorous line of Wilde's in which they arrive as with a roll of drums,

> And yet, and yet,
> Those Christs that die upon the barricades,
> God knows it, I am with them, in some things.

The qualification of support in the last three words suggests that one with a liking for a Pale Pink shade in politics is shying away from the true scarlet of the Red Flag. Such an evasion is as unfortunate as Shelley's hesitation concerning the whereabouts of his skylark, that blithe spirit, 'who, from heaven, or near it', poured out his profuse strains of unpremeditated art. 'Near it' may rhyme with spirit – or at least come near to doing so – but it will hardly bear thinking about as a contribution either to ethereal cartography or to poetry. Wilde, while apparently withdrawing from support of freedom's more combatant sons, made the most, musically, of the barricades and no line containing them is likely to go far wrong.

I have commented before on the assured poetic potency of a roll of a's, o's, and r's. The old form of barricade, barricado, naturally assists in producing this type of rat-a-plan. Wordsworth employed such percussion-music finely in his:

And sorrow, barricado'd evermore
Within the walls of cities,

Here barricado knocks powerfully on our ear-drums and at our feelings and the r's and w's continue to force an entrance to the heart and to build up a most pitiful picture of urban melancholy.

BENNET

I SUPPOSE that the common family name Bennett is a shortening of Benedict, the blessed one. In Turbervile's 'Heroycall Epistles', which are Ovidian translations and a source-book of the Tudor drama, I found Oenone reminding Paris of old and simple pleasures,

How oft have we in shaddow layne
  Whilst hungry flocks have fed?
How oft have we of grasse and groaves
  Prepar'd a homely bed?
How oft on simple stacks of straw
  And bennet did we rest?

What is this bennet? Well it is Herb Bennet (not a younger relation of Arnold Bennett's) and it puts the devil to flight. It may be Avens. It may be Hemlock. It may be Wild Valerian. Valerian, one of the later Roman Emperors, gave his name to a therapeutic herb 'with antispasmodic effects'. The proper medicine, then, for quite a number of contemporary poets and musicians. Would that some of our syncopators could withdraw to homely beds of grass and 'rest on bennet'!

BISHOP

WHAT an astonishing collection of meanings has bishop when used as a verb! To bishop is to confirm and to make a bishop of: these are natural enough. But 'to file down the teeth of a horse', and 'to murder by drowning' are odd indeed. So, by this token, Brides-in-the-Bath Smith was an episcopal type! *A Supplementary English Glossary* (1881) records that: 'In 1831 two men, Bishop and Williams, drowned an Italian boy in Bethnal Green in order to sell his body to the doctors.' Hence Bishop is a parallel to Burke and the two ride together in the *Ingoldsby Legends*. 'I Burked the Papa, now I'll Bishop the Son.' Another (still used) meaning is 'to let the milk burn while cooking'. This is explained by reference to former persecution and faggots long ago. 'If the porage be burned, we say the bishop hath put his foote in the potte because bishops burn who they lust.' Altogether a sinister verb and far from complimentary to our Doctors of Divinity.

BLANCH

I AM reminded of a phrase queer to us, occurring in Sir Henry Wootton's letter to Milton,

> Now, Sir, concerning your travels, wherein I may chalenge a little more privilege of Discours from you; I suppose you will not blanch Paris in your way; therefore I have been bold to trouble you with a few lines to Mr. M. B. whom you will easily find attending the young Lord S. as his Governour. . . .

Blanch here is blench, which is to blink, to start back, to edge away from, avoid, even bilk. I take it that blanching or blenching with fear does not mean going white, but making a run for it. But the similarity of the two kinds of blanch, the French blanch of pallor, and the Saxon blanch of blinking, bolting, has caused a natural confusion. A schoolboy who blanched the headmaster's study might have a certain greyness of aspect as he sneaked by. But Milton, if he did blanch Paris, could retain his normal colour as he did so. No nervous anaemia was implied.

BLOW

I HAVE been asked why blow no longer means blossom, except occasionally in the relics of rustic speech. Most of us, I suppose, think of the wild thyme stirred in the breeze when Oberon says that this herb 'blows' on the much-quoted bank. But Shakespeare's usage is made quite plain by

> As the most forward bud
> Is eaten by the canker e'er it blow.

Presumably Wordsworth still thought of the old meaning and referred to blooming when he wrote of 'the meanest flower that blows'; yet I must confess to having visualized in the past a nodding, swaying flower as the image that he had in mind. We keep the old blow in our adjectives, since over-blown means over-ripe and the noun blowen for a sluttish woman suggests to me a full-blown, over-ripe party, who has reached the petal-shedding phase of human existence. Addison used the noun blow almost as a verb of assembly when he wrote of 'a blow of tulips'. This is delightful. The departure from the old and blossomy meaning of blow seems to have been made in Victorian times.

BOANTHROPY

BOANTHROPY is the curious malady which befell Nebuchadnezzar, namely that of believing oneself to be an ox. But Nebuchadnezzar did more than believe; he became.

'The same hour was the thing fulfilled upon Nebuchadnezzar: and he was driven from men, and did eat grass as oxen, and his body was wet with the dew of heaven, till his hairs were grown like eagles' feathers and his nails like birds' claws.'

According to the poet:

> He murmured as he chewed the unwonted food,
> 'It may be wholesome but it is not good.'

If Nebuchadnezzar did have these doubts, the king was only a half-hearted boanthrope, for a true ox-man would have tucked in with avidity. All-in boanthropy is not, I think, very common nowadays. The profounder psychologists may argue that the assumption of the name of John Bull as a national symbol proved the presence of subconscious boanthropic tendencies among the English, but John Bull has ceased to be either an accurate or popular figure-head for our policy and mood. There are a few people who eat mainly grass and many who are content with salads and such; but there is no reason to dub Sir Stafford Cripps a boanthrope on that account; he might as well be labelled hippanthrope. Boanthropy was practised of old by some legendary deities for purposes of amour.

BODKIN

WE all know Hamlet's bare bodkin and the needle form of bodkin is still with us. But we have lost the passenger bodkin, which is foolish in this age of crowded transport and of rush-hour massing of bodies. A bodkin was a person wedged in between two others when there was room for two or two and a half at most. All three were lucky if the third party happened to be needle-thin. One might perhaps say in these times that the Liberal Party in Great Britain sits bodkin between the other two – and for a time, certainly, it had no more than needle-thickness. Thackeray has bodkin-sitters in the various forms of barouche which his characters use and every modern motorist and his passengers know the invader. This kind of bodkin turns up in Sydney Smith's definition of nicety in people.

'A nice person is neither too tall nor too short, looks clean and cheerful, has no prominent feature, makes no difficulties, is never misplaced, sits bodkin, is never foolishly affronted, and is void of affectations.'

The proper qualities then of a well-conducted bodkin are lack of bulk and presence of modesty, the former being especially essential. Those who, like myself, do not make the bodkin grade physically, have the satisfaction of being put in the front seat with the driver instead of afflicting the couple behind. When there were myriads of cars on the road bodkins were less common than they have been in Britain recently. When cars are made scarce by lack of petrol, we must use the accommodation to the full and so bodkinism inevitably increases. But the word has almost vanished.

BOGGART, ETC.

FEW of our practising poets have a richer vocabulary than Wilfrid Gibson who draws at will on the grand, racy lingo of the Northumbrian fells and Scottish Border where speech seems to make the best of both worlds, English and Scottish. His narrative poem 'Coldknuckles', reminiscent of John Masefield's early tales in octosyllabic rhyme, has a fine assemblage of sounding terms. Take this, for example, for the panic of a lad who has blundered into a burial ground:

> Cold prickles crawled up Isaac's back,
> Bristling his scalp, till, chittering,
> He would have given anything
> If only he might make a round
> And dodge that spooky burial ground:
> But in such fog he feared to quit
> The road, lest he should stray, and It,
> Through sluthery moss and clungy sump,
> Should track him until the last Trump –

The nameless shapeless Dread, that now
Dogged close at heel; though when, or how
The Thing had fallen in behind,
He could not tell; and, fleyed to find
His own fetch following, and learn
His doom of death, he dared not turn
His eyes to meet that grisly grin
Which sent cold shivers under his skin,
As, mimicking the way he walked,
Stealthily his own spectre stalked,
Fumbling chill fingers through his hair . . .
Then, all at once, the foggy air
Was ripped with ellerish yells and wails;
And boggles out of old wives' tales –
Brag, horney, hobthrush, wirrikow –
Were flaffering all about him now.
Skirl after skirl sang through the night,
Till he was bivvering with fright.

Chittering reminds me of boyhood bathing: on cold days we were given a bun on coming out of the water: it was called 'a chittering bit'.

A fetch is a long-drawn breath and hence, perhaps, an expiration. And does not expire suggest death? So fetch for wraith or apparition. That may be a dubious explanation, but the word is an apt one for a ghost.

Fley speaks, frighteningly, for itself. Ellerish is presumably eldritch. Boggarts and boggons remain common imps of the north and linger still in the geography of Manchester. Is brag some corruption of boggart?

Horney is the horned one, the devil, and so can stand for any of his spooky manifestations. Burns knew Auld Horney in Ayrshire. Hobthrush brings us back to England. Hob or Robin Goodfellow means either hobgoblin or wood-louse. Wirrikows are Border beasties and were known to Sir Walter. Also to Allan Ramsay, who puts them in his 'Elegy on Maggy Johnston':

Maggy Johnston liv'd about a Mile Southward of *Edinburgh*, kept a little Farm, and had a particular Art of brewing a small Sort of Ale agreeable to the Taste, very white, clear and intoxicating, which made People who lov'd to have a good Pennyworth for their Money be her frequent Customers. And many others of every Station, sometimes for Diversion, thought it no Affront to be seen in her Barn or Yard.

Maggy's small beer, surprisingly vodka-coloured, could apparently be potent and make a penny do the work of a pound today, for the poet confesses to growing 'sae fou' one summer night that, in a field, he sank down to take a night's 'Balillilow' (lullaby or nap).

And when the Dawn begoud to glow,
I hirsl'd up my dizzy Pow,
Frae 'mang the Corn like Wirricow,
  Wi' Bains sae sair,
And ken'd nae mair than if a Ew
  How I came there.

No doubt there are many more words lingering on the verge of dialect to suggest the boggart, fetch, hobthrush, horney, and wirrikow. But these will do to go on with. I surmise that the root of wirrikow is the same as that of war: that root was a comparatively mild origin for so dreadful a thing and meant only worry or confusion. A fetch might worry one and did, indeed, worry the small boy in Gibson's 'Coldknuckles', fully earning the grim, queer name of wirrikow.

BOSS

A BOSS, as we all know, is a protuberance, a knot, a jutty decoration. It is several other things as well, but I like it best as a protuberant person, especially a lady, 'grasse et grosse'. So, gloriously, it occurs in Marlowe's 'Tamburlaine' (Part I, III, 3). Zabina, wife of Bajazeth, says to Zenocrate,

Base concubine, must thou be placed by me
That am the Empress of the mighty Turk?

whereupon Zenocrate counters with a straight jab to the jaw,

Disdainful Turkess and unreverend boss,
Call'st thou me concubine, that am betrothed
Unto the great and mighty Tamburlaine!

The first of these lines is, in my opinion, a knock-out. Bajazeth and Zabina are continually alluded to in this play as King and Queen of bassoes.

BRANDLE

GERARD MANLEY HOPKINS revived brandle for hit or shake. The Scots have brangle in this sense. I take this to be a separate word for brandish, which is a verb derived from a noun. One brandished, originally, a brand, i.e. a sword or torch. Hopkins wrote in *The Bugler's First Communion*,

I have put my lips on pleas
Would brandle adamantine heaven, with ride and jar.

Brandle, I discover, can also mean to fortify or fuddle with brandy. The two uses might pleasantly collide if some Colonel Chinstrap were found carelessly brandling a glass or bottle, being himself already brandled. Certainly brandled is a more gentlemanly term than some such current usage as 'well ginned up'. If there were Baedeker markings for words, we might suitably give brandle three stars.

BRICK-BAT

FURTHER information on the brick-bat mystery. My (and others') interpretation of brick-bat as brick-bit, lump of brick, the

Cockney's 'arf-a-brick, is challenged. Herewith a correspondent's note. After saying that he had been well-entertained by my views on the subject, he said that this

> reminds me of the aged story of The Englishman, Frenchman, and German, who were asked to describe an elephant. The Englishman of course went out and shot one and brought home the body. The Frenchman wrote an essay on 'L'Eléphant et ses amours' and the German evolved a Camel from his inner consciousness. The Brown Brickbat is very Teutonic. I agree that a Brickbat ought to be as he described it, but it ain't. It is a very heavy weapon rather like the club of the giant Blunderbore. It was used for running down and levelling brick paving. Most stables and pigsties and yards were paved in brick when I was a child. It is not as big as the battle stone paviours used, but a more wieldy weapon.

But why were these brickbats used as missiles? They must have been unwieldy. Hammer-throwing and caber-tossing are forms of athletic exercise and means of rivalry, not of practical assault and militant battery.

BUCCANEER

DEFOE'S Captain Singleton spoke 'buccaneer words'. One might think from this allusion to wild speech that buccaneer had something to do with the Latin 'bucca', a cheek. The buccaneer would, in that case, be cousin to the buccinator, the man of puffed cheeks and a blower of the trumpet. But the buccaneer is oddly derived from the French hunters who cooked their meat on a buccan or wooden frame for camp use. So buccaneers became roaring adventurers of all kinds and later on were mainly maritime pirates: this is odd, since these were least likely to use the buccan in their cuisine.

Buccaneer is a good, roystering, reverberating word for the old bold mates of Henry Morgan, of whose desperado qualities Masefield sang so zestfully. I was lured to reading very early by the appeal of fiction's buccaneers, chief of whom, for me, was an appalling scoundrel called Gideon Lipchop. This admirable name has lingered in memory ever since. Gideon was an invention of a writer called S. Walkey, author of *Rogues of the Fiery Cross*. He held us spell-bound, week by week, in *Chums* – unless you waited and got the whole thing in one glorious gobbet by acquiring a bound volume at Christmas. I have often wondered about S. Walkey who thus lit up my early winters. What did S. stand for? It should have been something large and lurid, like Sebastian. Was he a tired man grinding out his 'buccaneer words' under duress? Or did Gideon give him joyous inspiration! At any rate these serialists of the juvenile weeklies are worshipped as few others. Now radio rules and Dick Barton holds the listening world in fee, overwhelming rather than performing roguery. I have entirely forgotten what righteous fellow finished Gideon's career of crime; once more virtue failed to be 'news'. It was Lipchop who lived on for me. Buccaneers, oh, buccaneers!

BUDGET

BUDGET comes from the Latin *Bulga* by way of bougette, knapsack. Bilge and Bulge are cousins, bilge being the broad part of a ship's bottom before the word was applied to the sloppy contents thereof. Budget is a queer, domestic little word for this mighty engine of taxation and expenditure which now handles thousands of millions of pounds every year. The Shakespearean mumbudget is an invocation to silence. Knapsack is peculiar. Knap means to snap, break, grind, as in flint-knapping: it is also to bite. So knapsack became the snack-bag, sandwich-budget, or bag for the 'baggins'.

BUG AND HUMBUG

THE kind of bug which interests me is the bogy-bug, first cousin to the boggart whom we have just discussed. When Hamlet, his sea-gown scarf'd about him in the dark, 'finger'd the packet' of those commissioned to grind an axe upon his head, he discovered many counterfeit pleas of State why this should be done. The dispatch was,

> Larded with many several sorts of reasons,
> Importing Denmark's health and England's too,
> With, ho! such bugs and goblins in my life.

Bug is here our bug-a-boo, a source of false alarm. Posthumus in *Cymbeline* has a striking phrase for those who strike terror in a battle. They are 'the mortal bugs o' the field'. Again in *3 Henry VI*, v, 2 there is a line which might be misunderstood:

> For Warwick was a bug that feared us all.

This does not mean that bugs could be fearful as well as fearsome; the verb fear is obviously transitive here and means frighten. *O.E.D.* quotes this line to prove that bug meant a fellow and was the source of the American usage 'Big bug' for a tycoon or 'big shot'. Bug may have been slang for chap in Elizabethan times, but far more commonly it is a bogy, fetch or wirrikow.

So on to bug-a-boo, bug-bear, and humbug. This last is a word which must often astonish foreigners at large in the English language. We are used to the look of it. How queer it must seem when met for the first time!

Did the word 'hum', meaning an imposture or to impose, come from 'hum-bug'? More probably it fathered it. So humbug begins as a false fear, a kinsman of Chimera, that medley of lion, goat, and serpent, killed by Bellerophon, who has been haunting leading articles in the English Press for many a year. Chimerical became a general adjective for fanciful, losing the idea of terror, while humbug was transferred from the world of scarecrow and fiend to that of moral impostor. The hypocrite began as a professional actor in Greece (no offence in the name) and came to mean a pretender anywhere. So the humbug begins as a spook or some such thing and then becomes a pretending spook; he at length ends up in the more solidly pretentious form of Mr. Pecksniff.

That hypocrisy can still be acting in a useful form and that humbug renders social service is a tenable belief. Lord Macmillan in an article on 'The Vogue of Humbug' certainly did not hold that point of view without very large qualifications; he was not condoning humbug when he quoted Sir Hugo Mallinger in *Daniel Deronda*: Sir Hugo counters the hero's expressed distaste for the shams of politics. 'A man,' he says, 'who sets his face against every sort of humbug is simply a three-cornered, impracticable fellow. There's a bad style of humbug, but there is also a good style, one that oils the wheels and makes progress possible. There is no action without a little acting.'

Concerning the bug of entomology, the Americans, as everyone knows, have kept the proper meaning and apply the word generally to grubs and insects. We have revived it for *Cimex Lectularius*, the pest of bed and board wherever cleanliness breaks down. The odious stench of its presence, quite apart from its painful onslaughts, is no bug-a-boo, but true terror to clean people.

BUNTER

WE heard much in England at one time about barrow-boys; this tribe of fruit-sellers swarmed in great numbers in certain streets, sometimes accused of over-charging, sometimes praised for keeping prices down by giving the shop-keepers keen and healthy competition. In general it was supposed that they might find something better to do at a time when productive labour was so greatly needed. Some were accused, with justice, of sharp practice, i.e. showing a few good apples or pears on top and filling your bag with damaged or over-ripe fruit from below: but others were fair dealers.

The barrowman is as old as commerce itself; and frequently it was the barrow-woman. I found this observation of Smollett's Matthew Bramble:

> It was but yesterday that I saw a dirty barrow-bunter in the street, cleaning her dusty fruit with her own spittle; and who knows but some fine lady of St. James's parish might admit into her delicate mouth those very cherries which had been rolled

and moistened between the filthy, and perhaps ulcerated, chops of a St. Giles's huckster?

Why bunter? A bunter was an eighteenth-century term for a woman who collected rags, but to bunt was also to push. A barrow-bunter was thus a barrow-pusher. It interested me to find this use of bunt, because when I was a very small boy and played Association Football (Rugby Football coming with larger years), charging or barging into another player was called by us bunting. I fancy that usage has disappeared: I never hear boys employing it now. Butt, as in butting out or butting into, is perhaps a variation.

Bunt is a word of numerous meanings. It is the middle part of a sail or fish-net. It is also a verb for hauling up the bunt of the sail. Then, we have the buntings which are 'insessorial birds', buntings which are shrimps, buntings which are terms of endearment (Baby Bunting does not refer to a pushful child), and bunting which is pieces of worsted used for flag-waggery. Possibly the group of avian buntings were so called because of their brown hue. Brown was originally burned or burnished. Were they 'burntings' or were they bunters in the perky, pushing, aggressive, sparrowy sense?

What an imposing word is this 'insessorial' which is used to define the buntings! It means perching. 'The Perchers have three toes in front and one behind adapted for perching on trees.' Are not some human beings naturally insessorial, whatever may be their toe-equipment? I once knew an old, dried up, scholastic fellow who looked so like a bat in a Natural History Museum that I could not believe that he ever went to bed at night: he must, I thought, just hang himself up on the wall. He typified a whole tribe of humans who are instinctively perchers. Chairs and sofas have no attraction for them: they always seem to be climbing on to some furniture of other function, tables, cupboards, or hot water pipes, for purposes of squatting. Such folk are apt to be called 'queer old coots', but they should, it seems, be termed Buntings, since that would sum up their perching ways and their habit of fidgeting and pushing the furniture about in order to be insessorial.

CARDIALGY

HEARTY things have become cordial in our language; we use the Latin word when something pleasant is implied. The unpleasantness has tended to remain Grecian and so to be cardiac. No lovers, I think, have so far complained of cardialgy or cardiopathy and a dramatist in search of his title naturally prefers 'Heartbreak House' to 'Cardialgic Mansion'. A medical correspondent, with a taste for the English language, mentions cardiopath with disgust.

> I object strenuously to the word 'biopsy' which has come into general use among doctors. It is supposed to be a sort of near relative to 'necropsy'. I object to the dreadful practice of American doctors using the word 'pathology' for 'disease'. I have read in an American medical journal an article headed 'Dietetics in Cardiopaths'. It was about food in heart disease. I hope you heard that the Minister of Education in a recent speech used the expression 'liquidation of illiteracy' for 'education'.

As a specimen of politicians' English my correspondent quotes 'Organizational preliminaries', when all that is meant is preparations.

I am with him on all points. But cardialgies and the like can at least plead that they sit in good company. There are some fine-sounding 'card' words, admittedly not cardiac, but warming to the heart. Cardamine, for the genus of plants including Lady-Smock or Cuckoo flower, is a handsome neighbour to Cardoon (a species of artichoke) and both have to fight Carduus, the thistle, and escape the attention of the Cardophagite, the almost omnivorous donkey who treats thistles as 'dietetics'. (Might not a schoolmaster thus break out, since indignation makes for verse. 'O monstrous dolt, long-eared cardophagite'?) Cardinals have been helped by their name and Cardigans seem to be heart-warming articles, though I do not suppose that the Welsh county of Cardigan owes its title to the heart. Nostalgic has been worked to death in our time for all backward-looking and regretful moods. Perhaps the critics who drag nostalgic into every sentence will now take up cardialgic to gratify their zest for the classics. 'This tragedy, soaring to the superb cardialgy of Act V.' No, it will not do. Heart-break is there for ever, a word that is a winter's tale in itself.

CLEM

No politics: but it did occur to me once or twice during Mr. Clement Attlee's command of affairs that clem means starve in the north of England, where starved very often means cold. In St. John Ervine's play *Private Enterprise* the rich and vacant-minded girl who has married a V.C. turned Labour Member says proudly of her new leader, 'We call him Clem – among ourselves of course. His name's Clement. After the saint, I think.' Clemency is a noun of some beauty, and clement is a fair adjective for merciful. But Clem is ugly and, if I were a Clement, I would hate to be 'Clemmed'.

Abbreviation of this kind, however harsh to the eye and the ear, is very popular. But can it be maintained that the monosyllables one hears all about one, Stan, Russ, Ran, Cliff, Ray and so on, are an improvement on the older and longer and almost feudal Stanley, Russell, Randall, Clifford, and Raymond? Players of games, especially professional players, have now 'clemmed' their Christian names to the barest bones. While watching an ice-hockey match not long ago I noticed how the young Canadians had trimmed their methods of nomination. Pete, Art, Gib, Bur, Bob, and Ab made up a good, curt sextet. We could especially admire Ab. Abe, of course, was such a mouthful, if Abraham was the original! But Ab may have been Abel, Abner, or Abimelech. The next team so listed named its heroes as Ken, Ran, Gar, Doug, and Don. No troublesome dissyllables there!

These brevities are certainly brief, but they are also vague. Ran, one presumes, is Randolph; but it might be Randall or Ranulph. Gar might be anything. Further reflections arise. What a deal of time King Arthur (or rather King Art), Tom Malory, Al Tennyson, and others would have saved if they had abbreviated in the modern fashion! Lance and Guine, Ene and Ger would have paired off nicely. Dag, Tris, Gaw, Mod, Bed, Merl, and Perce would have taken the same space round the table as did the longer-titled knights of old, but they would have required less breath and far less space in a line.

True, there is nothing novel about abbreviations, pet-names, and nicknames. But they are often curious. It is not odd that Jack arrived, but it is odd that he came from Johannes and not from Jacobus. Why did Henry yield Hal, Edward Ned, and Mary Molly? We need not puzzle too much, but we can sometimes approve. The old abbreviations were not unpleasant to the ear. But nowadays we seem to have no instinct for a gracious brevity. Of this fact Walter is a good example. The old-time Wat wins affection at once. But the moderns will not have it. We are always hearing of Wal and Wally, and they make one shiver. Recently I read of four famous brothers of a London family who had conquered Hollywood in some function. They were announced as Ern, Stan, Wal, and Perce. As Ernest, Stanley, Walter, and Percival I am sure that most of us would have liked them better. Besides, many of these clippings are so drastic as to be wholly vague. Does Wal stand for Walter, Wallace, Walmersley, Walpurgis, or what? Is the American Al an Alfred, an Albert, an Algernon, or an Algonquin?

So, I prefer Clement Attlee and Herbert Morrison to Clem and Herb (or Bert). Sir Stafford Cripps has defied the curtailers. You might call a Stafford Staff over a glass of beer, but not over a somewhat 'clemming' salad of raw cabbage and grated carrot!

One of the oddities of abbreviation is the class distinction involved. Staff, for example, sounds common as short for Stafford. But would not Staffie pass in higher circles? Bert and Reg are certainly not very high in social tone. But the Berties and Reggies can abound among what are still, so strangely, called 'club-men'. It is quite impossible to imagine a Bertie Wooster being called Bert at the Long Bar and there would never be a Reg, though there may be a Reggie, at Fogey's Club or Drones'.

COCKNEY

FRANCIS MERES quoted Sir Philip Sidney's somewhat cryptic saying, concerning vague-minded criticism and muddled dislike: 'Many cockney and wanton women are often sick, but in faith they cannot tell where; so the name of poetry is odious to some.' Sidney further mentioned the difficulty of giving any 'Fast handle' to such 'carping dispraise'. Obviously this cannot be our Cockney, the Londoner who drew his name from the Kingdom of Cockaigne, once an imaginary abode of ignorance and idleness. The early Cockney of the English language was a cockered (or spoiled, petted, and so queasy) person. What exactly did Shakespeare mean by the word cockney? He used it twice and both times gave it to a clown. 'I fear this great lubber the world will prove a cockney,' says Feste. The Fool in *King Lear* exclaims, 'Lay to it, nuncle, as the cockney did to the eels when she put 'em i' the paste alive: she knapp'd them o' the coxcombs with a stick and cried, Down, wantons, down.' Cockney to the Fool is a woman, and the word is linked, as in Sidney, with wanton. So the idea of a fussy, finical wench is implied, the opposite of a lubber. Cockneys have much changed their status with the centuries.

COMITY

ONLY recently did I realize that comity does not mean a group of *comites*, which is Latin for companions. It had struck me as a charming word for fellowship, so much more elegant and gracious than committee. Probably most people fancy that the comity of nations is a rhetorical phrase used by indignant or uplifted Foreign Secretaries to signify the company of nations. But comity is courtesy and the comity of nations is defined by Chambers as 'the international courtesy by which effect is given to the laws of one state within the territory of another'. Bacon linked comity with honest behaviour and affability. But would a pastor or master of today, who rebuked the young for lack of comity, be understood? I think not. The mistaken use of comity has now prevailed so far as to oust the old meaning altogether. Some perusal of leading articles has led me to think of a comity purely as a group. It is a pity, because comity is a fair word and to tell or read of a good man's comity of living would come agreeably to the ear and eye.

COWSLIP

'THE dungy earth', not the moist mouth of a cow, entitles both cowslip and oxlip. Old English slyppe was a dropping, slimy and viscous, and presumably both these cousins of the spring were supposed to flourish where ox and cow had passed. The oxlip, defined as intermediate between cowslip and primrose, was 'bold' in Shakespeare's opinion: the cowslip yellow and freckled. To Milton they were 'Cowslips wan that hang the pensive head', and in *Comus* he described the head as velvet. Matthew Arnold linked cowslips with Cumnor, Kipling with Devon.

> Violets of the Undercliff
>   Wet with Channel spray,
> Cowslips from a Devon combe
>   Midland furze afire,
> Buy my English Posies
>   And I'll sell you hearts' desire.

Hood called cowslip 'a country wench', which was obvious. Gay said that she 'paints the shining' field, which takes us back to Shakespeare and the meadows painted with delight. The finest thing ever written of cowslips was also (naturally) by Shakespeare, when he further defined the freckling of the flower. Of the sleeping Imogen, it was said:

> On her left breast
> A mole cinque-spotted, like the crimson drops
> I' the bottom of a cowslip.

Why evolution threw these crimson (or to me brownish-orange) drops into the bell where Ariel loved to lie, who shall say? But we count them at the end of April with gladness, whatever the tint. From slime-droppings to Imogen and Ariel! Here's the upward march indeed, a floral dance from dungy earth to air and ecstasy.

CRINOLINE AND MILLINER

THE crinoline has always seemed to me a well-named article. It enters a sentence with a nice genteel swing, a bobbing elegance. I owe to James Laver the reminder that 'the French for horse-hair is crin and a hundred years ago women began to wear little pads of crin on their hips to make them look larger and to give a proper fall to the all-growing voluminousness of their skirts. The end of that process was the crinoline'.

Many of our wardrobe words come from place-names. The cambrics and calicos declare their origin: I was surprised to learn that milliner came from Milan, and meant at first anybody who dealt in the nick-nacks of 'ingenious Italy'. The limitation to hats came much later. Milliner always reminds me of the popinjay staff-officer whom Shakespeare's Hotspur so amusingly ridiculed. This exquisite of the battle-field held that vulgar corpses should not be brought 'betwixt the wind and his nobility'. As Hotspur put it,

> But I remember, when the fight was done,
> When I was dry with rage and extreme toil,
> Breathless and faint, leaning upon my sword,
> Came there a certain lord, neat, and trimly dress'd,
> Fresh as a bridegroom; and his chin new reap'd
> Show'd like a stubble-land at harvest-home;
> He was perfumèd like a milliner;
> And 'twixt his finger and his thumb he held
> A pouncet-box, which ever and anon
> He gave his nose, and took't away again.

Such was, for a while, the English opinion of Milanese finery and its representatives.

Another odd arrival has been cravat which is Croatian. The type of man dismissed as a scented milliner would later on have been cravatted about the neck. Later still he would have designed the head-wear for the crinolined ladies. Had these last chosen sprigged muslin, they would have been drawing on Mosul. For our muslin is a Middle-Eastern invader.

CRONY

THE crony comes in with Pepys. The age of Charles II, says Bernard Groom in his *Short History of English Words*, was prodigal of brevities. The Restoration dramatists liked some stately terms too, but it seems that

> Short informal words are the characteristic contribution of the time to our language. Banter and crony are first recorded in the reign of Charles II. Sham appears about 1677, and was much used during the excitement of the Popish Plot. The abusive term Whig was applied to the promoters of the Exclusion Bill in 1679 and was soon the accepted badge of a great political party. Prig came into use as 'a vague term of disrespect' about the same time. Chum is first recorded in 1684, fun in 1685, mob in 1688. Swift protested against the spread of new popular words,[1] especially against the 'barbarity which delights in monosyllables'. But there seems to have been small opposition to the movement until the great campaign against 'low' language in which both Johnson and Chesterfield played an energetic part.

Crony I find particularly fascinating. It suggests a certain snuffling guile, a companionship in mischief, a joint pottering over the cups and glasses; it smells of gossip and of 'another one for the road'.

Burns so used it to perfection.

> His ancient, trusty, drouthy crony:
> Tam lo'ed him like a vera brither,
> They had been fou for weeks thegither.

[1] 'I have done my utmost to stop the Progress of Mobb and Banter' (Swift).

Drouthy, so much better than thirsty, and fou, so much more suggestive than full, run nicely with crony. The *Oxford English Dictionary* calls it University slang, but the crony soon widened his social range and I think of the Dublin soaks, saloon-bound fellow-travellers, as cronies. Was not Joxer Daly a perfect crony for the Peacock?

Cronies appear to be exclusively male and have nothing to do with aged crones. There is no reason, except chance association, why they should be spoken of as old. May we not have young cronies? Surely a University word should have some relevance to the friendships of one-and-twenty. Nowadays the young appear to have their buddies; and cronies are getting scarcer too. But they must not disappear.

CURIOSO

CURIOSO may be well-nigh extinct, but he is as good a fellow, surely, as the virtuoso who survives almost in abundance. A curioso took care, inquired, studied, was expert. He practised curiosity in Dr. Johnson's sense. 'Curiosity is, in great and generous minds, the first passion and the last.' The curioso loved that into which he probed. He was a lover of the rare and queer as well as learned therein, the true amateur. The usage of 'curious' to describe books of an abnormal or indecent kind – as the bookseller judges indecency – is a common feature of certain literary catalogues. This links, in a one-sided way, with the activities of a curioso. But the true curioso had a wider range of taste.

Curiosity has declined in status. It is now a synonym for tiresome inquisitiveness; nursemaids – when there were such – used to observe, for what reason I do not know, that 'curiosity killed the cat' and so implied that small people practising the first and last passion of great and generous minds were reprehensibly engaged and well on the way to the everlasting bonfire, in short Nosey Parkers (who, by the way, was this Prodnose Parker that he should have become immortal?)

I must admit a liking for Nosey as an adjective of dismissal. It is an expressively odious term for those extremely odious people who must ever be reading postcards, looking over shoulders, poking into desks and drawers, and badgering one with a flow of why's and where's and when's. The Curioso I visualize standing silent upon a peak of Helicon, viewing, discerning, subtly exploring. He is at the top of that high school in which the gabbling Nosey Parker is bottom of the lowest form.

Curious nowadays means, nearly always, strange or queer. Chaps and happenings of no importance are often curious. The word has lost quality and one is visited by a shiver of delighted surprise when it is once again met in exalted places, lurking, for example, among Marvell's greenest shades in the garden of Nun Appleton:

> What wondrous life is this I lead!
> Ripe apples drop about my head;
> The luscious clusters of the vine
> Upon my mouth do crush their wine;
> The nectarine and curious peach
> Into my hands themselves do reach:
> Stumbling on melons as I pass,
> Insnar'd with flowers I fall on grass.'

Why 'curious peach'? Was the peach seeking something in the poet's hands or just a rare, unusual fruit? In either case Marvell became, in the tranquil Fairfax home near Tadcaster, the curioso and virtuoso of all orchard thoughts or lawn philosophy.

CURRY

I HAD thought that currying favour was some sort of metaphorical cousin to the currying of meat. But, on reflection, I found this currying of favours so odd a phrase that I had to look into its origin. Then I discovered that I had been wrong from the start. Curry, i.e. 'meat or fish, cooked with bruised spices or turmeric', is simply an Anglicization of the Tamil Kari. There is another curry, which is a form of quarry and means the portion of a hunted animal given to the hounds. Finally, there is curry (of the stable) to rub, comb, dress, and so, proceeding from horse to man, to wheedle or flatter. Falstaff talked of 'currying with Master Shallow'. But why curry favours? This strange phrase seems to have come from a complete mistake. Fauvel or favel was a fallow horse which was supposed to be cunning and needed skilful approach. To curry favel was to be an adroit groom. Somebody misheard and misconstrued the term and so started the currying of favours.

I remember once thinking aloud what curried favours would taste like and being met with the excellent reply – I think from John Van Druten – 'Very like minced matters'. That set us devising a menu after this form, i.e. a menu in which all the items had a kitchen or a larder participle or adjective attached to some non-edible (or rarely edible) object. I have been trying to recall the result. For hors d'œuvre there might be Bottled, Soused, or Pickled Topers. For entrée, Minced Matters or Curried Favours. For game, Jugged and Grilled Prisoner. (Too cannibalistic?) For sweet, Poached Preserves with Buttered Catches and Candied Opinions. For savoury, Opponents on Toast. (Cannibalism again!) Candied Opinions, being a pun, is, I suppose, cheating and should be withdrawn. Those in search of another Paper Game can now set to work and draw up further menus.

CYPRESS

TENNYSON may not have been in his finest 'In Memoriam' form when he wrote:

> I see thee sitting crown'd with good,
> A central warmth diffusing bliss
> In glance and smile, and clasp and kiss,
> On all the branches of thy blood;

Thy blood, my friend, and partly mine;
For now the day was drawing on,
When thou should'st link thy life with one
Of mine own house, and boys of thine

Had babbled 'Uncle' on my knee;
But that remorseless iron hour
Made cypress of her orange flower,
Despair of hope, and earth of thee.

But the last two lines have the true quality of a poem which I am sufficiently old-fashioned to find magnificent in phrase and patterned rhythm; this, although I am less affected than most by its philosophy. 'Made cypress of her orange flower' is a poignant image. Cypress, though rather a 'hissy' word and awkward on the lips, is associated with so much black beauty that one quivers a little at the sight of it in poetry. It is Death's decoration and its symbol: it throws the shade and it makes the coffin. Walking in Greece one sees it as the finger of doom handsomely admonishing a sunlit landscape as it bursts into the burning life of an Hellenic April. The hard, bright air and the mistless horizon – so strange to the cloud-accustomed English eyes – define the cypress with astonishing clarity. Small wonder that its fine severity of silhouette seemed to haunt all idle singers of the idle day.

It stands sepulchral in the songs of Shakespeare.

Come away, come away, death
In sad cypress let me be laid.

Nothing of D. H. Lawrence's poetry is more widely remembered than his funeral piece:

All along the avenue of cypresses
All in their scarlet cloaks and surplices
Of linen, go the chanting choristers.

And cypress rears its crest, with lethal irony, in a brief, bitter rhyme by Douglas Young:

The Minister said it wald dee,
the cypress-buss I plantit.
But the buss grew til a tree,
naething dauntit.
It's growan, stark and heich,
derk and straught and sinister,
kirkyairdie-like and dreich,
But whaur's the Minister?

Young, defending his use of Plastic Scots, adds a note which traces the cypress beyond the Greek cuparissos to the gardens of the Cretan palaces. He says this of his vocabulary:

> I admit, to be sure, that the word 'Minister' is a Latin word, and that Dunbar and Henryson would have said 'Priest'. I agree that 'Cypress' is a word derived through French from some pre-Hellenic 'Minoan' tongue. But I deny that these plastically amalgamated gobbets of language bear not the remotest relation to any form of Scots current today. If that be so, why should farmers on a market-day in Cupar poke me in the ribs and ask 'Whaur's the Minister?'

Cuparissos – Cupar. Odd that his Cypress poem should just there be so much enjoyed. But anywhere in Scotland jokes about corpses seem to be enjoyed. Scottish humour, when it is not being farmyairdie-like and sexual, returns to the bottle – or the cadaver. This point Walter Elliot made to me during the first night of James Bridie's *Dr. Angelus*, a play,

derk and straught and sinister,
kirkyairdie-like and dreich.

The programme might have carried a small picture of a cypress.

DANDIPRAT, ETC.

A DANDIPRAT suggests at first a prattling dandy, a gossiping fop or macaroni. But it is nothing so substantial. It merely means anything little. It began as a small coin and ended as a small boy.

This form of urchin lurks in the by-ways of Elizabethan drama and makes one of his last appearances – for where is the imp now? – in Calverley's glorious piece of mock-Browning, 'The Cock and The Bull'. Speaking of his pebble-stone the poet proclaims:

> Well, to my muttons. I purchased the concern,
> And clapt it i' my poke, having given for same
> By way o' chop, swop, barter or exchange –
> 'Chop' was my snickering dandiprat's own term –
> One shilling and fourpence, current coin o' the realm.

This chop, term so dear to the snickering dandiprat, is cousin to chap and cheap, the market terms which gave us chapman, Cheapside, and the several Chippings of our English countryside, Chipping Norton, Chipping Sodbury, Chipping Ongar, and the like. Dandiprats, especially of the snickering kind, are much given to a crude form of chop-logic, which means exchange of argument. 'Chop and change' did not originally, I suppose, mean veer about or waver, but swop and barter.

Calverley, having introduced his dandiprat, continues to spray the reader with a rich jet of the 'classicalese' so dear to Browning:

> I shoved the timber ope wi' my omoplat;
> And *in vestibulo*, i' the lobby to-wit,
> (Iacobi Facciolati's rendering, sir,)
> Donn'd galligaskins, antigropeloes,
> And so forth; and, complete with hat and gloves,
> One on and one a-dangle i' my hand,
> And ombrifuge (Lord love you), case o' rain,
> I flopp'd forth, 'sbuddikins! on my own ten toes,
> (I do assure you there be ten of them),
> And went clump-clumping up hill and down dale
> To find myself o' the sudden i' front o' the boy.
> Put case I hadn't 'em on me, could I ha' bought
> This sort-o'-kind-o'-what-you-might-call toy,
> This pebble-thing, o' the boy-thing? Q.E.D.
> That's proven without aid from mumping Pope,
> Sleek porporate or bloated Cardinal.

Omoplat is shoulder-blade and ombrifuge umbrella. Of antigropeloes I have already written: they are water-defiers, mainly for the legs, and so are galligaskins, which were trousers or gaiters of the Grecian mode. Nowadays, those who wish to see ombrifuge, antigropeloes and galligaskins in their most protective, voluminous, and even colourful form should watch our leading golfers plodding through the downpour in some grim competitive event, from which none may flinch, however terrible the 'on-ding' of the elements, as a Scot would say. Golfers of this calibre know all about antigropelistic wrapping up.

What is the mumping Pope? Mumping can be either muttering or spongeing and cheating. Porporate I had to hunt out in the larger *O.E.D.* It is 'clad in purple'.

Of all these terms I would most like dandiprat to return to us. It is a darling word.

DAPPLE

SPOT is a mean little word and may refer to a nasty little thing. Dapple is a sweet word and is reserved, by the tact of language, for pleasant articles. Who has ever described an invalid as dappled with sores? The deer of Arden were dappled fools, not spotty ones, or, more scientifically, maculate morons. (Or should it be mora?) Dappled has won its enduring praise in those lines of Gerard Manley Hopkins which are now, I suppose, his best known. Thanking God for dappled things he included among life's particular benefits the wind-hover or 'dapple-dawn-drawn falcon', and of course,

> Rose-moles all in stipple upon trout that swim;
> Fresh-firecoal chestnut-falls; finches' wings;
> Landscape plotted and pieced – fold, fallow, and plough;
> And all trades, their gear and tackle and trim.

Certainly the dappled ones from leopard to thrush and trout have their fascination enhanced by the ripple of their epithet. We have dapple-grey horses too and skies dappled by the rise or set of sun. (Hopkins's 'skies of couple-colour as a brinded cow').

> Good morrow, masters; put your torches out:
> The wolves have prey'd; and look, the gentle day,
> Before the wheels of Phoebus, round about
> Dapples the drowsy east with spots of grey.
> Thanks to you all, and leave us: fare you well.

That is the kind of line that profusely dapples *Romeo and Juliet* and *A Midsummer Night's Dream*. But this quotation is from *Much Ado*. Both dapple and freckle have Nordic origins. I like them. Some people seem oddly fond of freckles. I have just read of a New York competition offering prizes for those children who can show the greatest number of freckles per square inch of skin. Hopkins might have thought this carrying his dapple-devotion rather far. It would be a short move onward to found a tournament of pimples for the adolescent.

DEBAUCHED

DEBAUCHED means, essentially, no more than lured aside or led astray. But what a glorious mouthful it is! I was caused to reflect on this by reading an advertisement in the first number of the *Observer*, December 4th, 1791, of 'a pleasing novel' to be issued in two volumes at five shillings.

> MEMOIRS of Julia de M——, a Country Girl, From the French of Le Chevalier Rutledge, Author of 'La Quinzaine Anglaise'. — 'Was not the fame of the Chevalier Rutledge already apparent as a pleasing writer, as a nice observer of human nature in all her forms, the present work would stamp his reputation. The progressive steps of Julia, from innocence to ruin, are but too natural; and while we admire the noble character of the Englishman, we cannot help pointing out that of the debauched Madam Champville as one whom all young women should avoid.' Journ. Encyclopédique.

The last opinion that ruin is all too natural to innocent young ladies can be disputed: but that the debauched Madam was one to be 'avoided' seems beyond argument. The last phrase, indeed, is masterly in its understatement. I have no doubt that the ingenious Chevalier proved his case and delighted his readers.

Debauched is even more attractive when spelt as deboshed. 'Thou deboshed fish', said Trinculo to Caliban and a haddock or skate in moral collapse is a wondrous thought. Finally, who can resist a debauchee? It is exactly the word to end an eighteenth-century sentence. 'So closed, with a resounding infamy, the career of this elegant debauchee?'

The seventeenth-century gossip and biographer, Aubrey, recorded of Shakespeare that 'he would not be debauched'. If invited to partake of debauchery William wrote that he was in pain. Debauched to Aubrey was not the adjective it became later. For him it meant 'led astray'; i.e. Shakespeare, when writing, was not to be diverted by invitations to parties.

DILETTANTE AND DILLITANT

SIR MAX BEERBOHM has written: 'Well, for my own part I am a dilettante, a petit maître. I love best in literature delicate and elaborate ingenuities of form and style. But my preference does not keep me from paying due homage to Titanic force and delighting, now and again, in its manifestation. I wonder at Ouida's novels and I wonder still more at Ouida.' We, too, may wonder sometimes at the extent to which 'Max' would carry his dilettantism and his cult of verbal elaboration, as, for example, when he described the racing of jockeys on the turf, as 'the scud-a-run of quivering homuncules over the vert on horses'. It was astonishing that, having striven so industriously not to use an ordinary word, he should at last have mounted anything so normal as a mere horse. What has so common a beast to do with 'the vert'? Surely the homuncules might have been poised on palfreys! (The palfrey, so dear to the romantic author of my youth, was a light saddle-horse contrasted with the heavy war-horse).

The dilettante is, properly, one who delights, and who more

delightful than such a man in our world which is so often either a dormitory of the lethargic or a cock-pit of the captious? But the name was diminished to mean one who took delight in trifles, a finical fellow, an amateurish idler among the arts. Indeed, it has become, unfortunately, a word of abuse. Pronounced in various ways by the enthusiasts of energy, it is now employed to hint disgust with the play-boy. I have heard a public speaker announce, with regard to politics, 'We want no dillitants in our movement'. (That was his version of the term.) Dillitant, with its suggestion of dilly-dally and hesitant, has surely a claim to incorporation, with honour, in the English language. The idea of delight and self-indulgence is still vaguely there along with that of inertia. Yes, on the whole, dillitant is an admirable word, and I fancy that 'Max' might gratefully accept it.

Carlyle had a good smack at the dillitants when he thundered:

> Midas-eared Mammonism, double-barrelled Dilettantism, and their thousand adjuncts and corollaries, are *not* the Law by which God Almighty has appointed His Universe to go.

Carlyle was uncommonly sure of himself and of his comprehension of God's Will. What exactly he meant by the adjective double-barrelled in this connection is hard to say. But at least we may surmise that Sir Max Beerbohm was never more than single-barrelled in his dillitancy.

DRUMLIE

THIS word just pushes its northern neb into the English dictionary. It means dark, turbid, muddied.

> The spate runs drumlie and broun
> Whummlan aathing doun.

Douglas Young in two lines pierces to the heart of the glen; the colour-scheme of a burn after rain is sombrely, faithfully pictured, 'drumlie and broun'. Drumlie is also applied to the minds and methods of those whom I have called the pudderers, the dealers in cultural or metaphysical or theological jargon. To compare them with a Scottish spate is, no doubt, complimentary. But I, when young, certainly was forced to sit under some drumlie pastors and masters and I was glad to find the word used of them by Dr. Ramsay in his *Reminiscences of Scottish Life and Character*.

> What mere English word could have expressed a distinction so well in such a case as the following? I heard once a lady in Edinburgh objecting to a preacher that she did not understand him. Another lady, his great admirer, insinuated that probably he was too 'deep' for her to follow. But her ready answer was, 'na, na, he's no just deep, but he's drumlie'.

Scottish also has the verb drumble for to make muddy or to confuse. Can it be intransitive also? So many speakers and writers could properly be described as 'drumbling away'.

DUMBARTON

ON being asked why a child's behind should be called a Dumbarton in Nursery Scottish, I referred the matter to Moray McLaren to whom I happened to be writing on loftier matters. Moray remembered the term as being used in his childhood and added:

> The word 'Dumbarton' is used for bottom in Scotland – or at least it was in my childhood. Both my wife and myself remember its use. It springs from the nurseries of that now almost extinct class – the Scottish Upper Middle or professional walk of life.
>
> Its origin is obviously a polite and euphonic evasion of the word bum. It is a refinement of evasion to add a syllable or two to a word you don't want to say, but to hint at, 'Christopher Columbus' for Christ, 'Goodness' for God, 'Jehoshaphat' or 'Jesophat' for Jesus, and so on.

This lengthening is a peculiar aspect of decorum. First the rhyme and then the extension. Nowadays, we are less fussy. 'Little Mary' died long ago and it seems incredible that anybody should ever have bothered to call trousers 'unmentionables'. It is possible, as my friend further supposed, that the prominence of the famous Dumbarton Rock suggested, by its aspect, a jutty behind, and that closeness (at the Clyde's bottom end) to 'the tail of the Bank' had something to do with it. But I can hardly believe that this is really so. The elongated rhyme is the best explanation. Dumbarton is, in any case, a picturesque result of prim evasiveness.

DUMBLEDOR

THE bumble-bee or the cock-chafer. Obviously the right word for a sleepy, summer afternoon, and murmurous shades. Also right for slow motion. It flits with Macbeth's drowsy hummer, the shard-borne beetle. That leads me to beetle as a verb of motion, a verb now most popular in schoolboy slang. I have surmised elsewhere that beetling about implies a tardy progress, a dumbledorish and deliberate gait or flight. But the parent of a boy who has 'beetle off' ever upon his lips advises me that 'beetling' is hurrying. 'A frantic scamper', he suggests, 'with all six legs working furiously. I think it's the basement beetle that's visualized, not the dumbledor.' Perhaps, but if I go a-beetling, I think I dally.

EMBER

EMBERS are well-named for warmth. (Why then Ember Days for appointments with austerity and the fastings of the faithful?) Any word which closely unites m, b and r starts with a useful advantage. Even when the other letters are not propitious, the result may yet be moving. Is not the place-name Gumber a comedian's asset, almost a grotesque, next door to Hogsnorton? Yet somehow it can emerge, just because of its constituent letters, with as much persuasion on the ear and the emotions as Vallombrosa itself. Take this, of Hilaire Belloc's,

Lift up your hearts in Gumber, laugh the Weald,
And you, most ancient valley of Arun, sing.
Here am I homeward from my wandering,
Here am I homeward, and my heart is healed.
If I was thirsty, I have heard a spring,
If I was dusty, I have found a field.

Even Gumber helps. It is far from prosaic. It has the warmth of embers in its middle. It is a common-place that remember is the grant-in-aid offered by the English language to every songster in search of his past and every devotee of the backward glance. Remember is reverberant, cordial, soothing. The difference between remember and recollect is that between poetry and prose. (It was in prose that Wordsworth defined poetry as 'the spontaneous overflow of powerful feelings: it takes its origin from emotion recollected in tranquillity'. It is surprising, even so, that he did not write 'remembered in tranquillity'). 'Recollect now thy Creator.' No, it will not do. Remembrance spreads beauty without effort. 'Remembered summer shines across the grass.' An exquisite line! Belloc again.

Remember is easy magic for the writer; to make quotation of its spell would fill a volume. But it is worth noting what strong service the 'ember' termination has rendered to three of our months, two of which are famous for unkindly weather. It has, as far as language can do it, caught the russet glow of ripening apples and of leaves on their way to the autumnal bonfire. It has made our Fall a festival of ember days in the warm and comforting sense and redeemed even November and December from ugliness, if not from sadness. Hood could rail at the former,

No warmth, no cheerfulness, no healthful ease,
No comfortable feel in any member,
No shade, no shine, no butterflies, no bees,
No fruits, no flowers, no leaves, no birds, November!

But the last line, while assisting with the play on words, does not really help him. November, despite all associations of fog and darkness, is a reassuring noise. January, the 'black Janiveer' of the

West Country, has a far less kindly sound. And February is justly harsh too.

> Good morrow, Benedick! Why, what's the matter
> That you have such a February face,
> So full of frost, of storm, and cloudiness?

Perhaps Shakespeare was finishing *Much Ado* at the end of a particularly loathsome February. It can hardly have been as dreadful as Britain's February of 1947, which was made the more oppressive by the shortage of embers and by the failure also of those imitation embers which the artificers of gas and electricity companies delight, in normal circumstance, to provide and to supply with heat.

Give December a chance and it has a warmth of its own,

> These two – they dwelt with eye on eye,
> Their hearts of old have beat in tune,
> Their meetings made December June
> Their every parting was to die.

Not even in the Brontë country does December emerge wholly bleak:

> Cold in the earth – and fifteen wild Decembers,
> From those brown hills, have melted into spring.

The word December has already started, by its own sound, a kind of thaw.

The chilliest December is in Shakespeare's Sonnet and certainly one blenches at,

> How like a winter hath my absence been
> From thee, the pleasure of the fleeting year!
> What freezings have I felt, what dark days seen!
> What old December's bareness everywhere!

Yet on the whole December, especially since it is assisted to a social warmth by the Christmas Festival and logs of Yule, is not a frightening or a bitter name. It has no east wind in its composition.

The embers glow. But nothing burns in February, save the fever which names the odious month and a fever is a hideous paradox, being cold heat and shiversome ardour.

EMPERY

HAS Empery, 'the power, status, or dominion of an Emperor', become entirely 'poetese'? In a leading article it would look a trifle odd. But odd things do remain in leading articles. Why, for example, do the composers of these exhortations still deal in 'behoving'? 'It now behoves the nation, etc.' Would the writer, on returning home, tell his wife that it behoved her to have a less deplorable supper on the table?

Does it behove us to keep empery in use? It is the kind of word that most modern poets detest. But then they probably detest these lines of Masefield's:

> In some green island of the sea,
> Where now the shadowy coral grows
> In pride and pomp and empery
> The courts of old Atlantis rose.
>
> In many a glittering house of glass
> The Atlanteans wandered there;
> The paleness of their faces was
> Like ivory, so pale they were.

The quatrains have, for me, an agreeable sea-music, as of waves lapping gently on the coral. Stewart Perowne insists that the green island must be Barbados, the only coralline contributor to the Caribbean archipelago. But surely Masefield had Bermuda in mind? That is a supposed site of Atlantis. Or perhaps he was not being strictly geographical at all. Archipelago was first a sea with many islands, especially the Aegean Sea, and then was applied to the islands themselves. Archipelagian makes a sounding and imposing adjective most suitable to apply to the isles of Greece. If Gibbon had written of the Decline and Fall of Athens he might well have described the downward drift of her archipelagian empery.

FANTASTIC

A GERMAN colleague of mine, who writes better English than most Englishmen do, habitually spells fantastic as phantastic. He is, in his way, correct. For do we not observe the Grecian origin by writing phantom instead of fantom? Phantom and yet fantasy! How does any foreigner ever grapple with the fantastic complications of our spelling? Fantastic comes to us through the classical phantasia, which chiefly means a vision, nightmare, hallucination. (Hallucination itself is an odd one, arriving in our language with an additional 'h' and 'l' from the (Ciceronian) Latin alucinor, I wander in mind.) I have always been fascinated by the word fantastic, because of the superb usage which Shakespeare gave to it. Bolingbroke, exiled by Richard II, is rather feebly comforted by John of Gaunt with,

> All places that the eye of heaven visits
> Are to a wise man ports and happy havens.

Whereupon the man doomed to wander exclaims, with some justice,

> O, who can hold a fire in his hand
> By thinking on the frosty Caucasus?
> Or cloy the hungry edge of appetite
> By bare imagination of a feast?
> Or wallow naked in December snow
> By thinking on fantastic summer's heat?

Fantastic here wonderfully suggests the heat-haze which lightly dances on a scorching day and creates illusive shapes over meadows and streams. Could any one word better render the essence of a summer landscape in three syllables?

Ophelia, going to the willowy brook ('There with fantastic garlands did she come'), was parted from reason when she made the sad journey. Fantastic here is more than merely strange: it has the touch of madness in it.

Fantastics and fantasticoes were common characters and butts of the Elizabethans. They were apish followers of foreign fashions, slightly daft as the plain man on the Bankside would see them. 'The pox of such antic, lisping, affecting fantasticoes' cried Mercutio, who deemed it lamentable that men of sense like himself should be afflicted with folk like Tybalt, these 'strange flies, these fashion-mongers, these pardonnez-mois'. Osric, a Danish fantastico, was likened to a water-fly, presumably the dragon-fly, which is not so named by Shakespeare. One of the most 'fantastic' flights of dragon-flies I ever saw was in 'fantastic summer's heat' where the Stour runs into Avon. The humid air above the water was full of a gleaming saraband of winged dancers made to seem yet more magical by the quivering of the atmosphere.

Fantastic has dwindled to mean strange or even shameful. Absurd situations, preposterous demands, exorbitant prices – these now carry the epithet which Shakespeare so typically and so beautifully employed to signify the conjuring tricks of Nature. He had a rare eye for all such fantasy.

> Sometime we see a cloud that's dragonish;
> A vapour sometime, like a bear or lion,
> A tower'd citadel, a pendant rock,
> A forked mountain, or blue promontory
> With trees upon't, that nod unto the world,
> And mock our eyes with air: thou hast seen these signs;
> They are black vesper's pageants.

I have been reminded (and *O.E.D.* supports the theory) that the verb to pant is of the same origin as fantastic. A nightmare sets us gasping. The popular or slang Latin phantasiare meant, as our slang has it, to 'get the willies', to 'get the wind up', and thus came to give us pant. Here is a strange course of arrival for the verb which gasps with thirst in 'As pants the hart for cooling streams'. That line is itself reminiscent of 'fantastic summer's heat' and all its quivering quality which 'nods unto the world and mocks our eyes with air'.

FANTIQUE

THIS word lingers on, at least among some families, meaning 'a spot of bother', as perhaps the younger members of those families would now, less elegantly, call it. Fantiques or fantads are, presumably, cousins of fantasy or fantastic. They began by meaning whims or crotchets and then were applied to the trouble which crochets may cause. To Sam Weller such fantiques, with a rougher spelling, were familiar. When he noisily entered Mr. Winkle's room in the Bush Hotel, Bristol, he attacked him with these remarks among others: 'Yon is an amicably disposed young man, Sir, I don't think, to go inwolwing our precious governor in all sorts o' fanteegs wen he's made up his mind to go through everything for principle. You're far worse nor Dodson, Sir, and as for Fogg, I consider him a born angel to you.' Fantiques and fanteegs have a close resemblance to the soldier's wearisome fatigues, but the first form, fantique, has a certain aristocratic flavour. Sam Weller might talk of fanteegs, but if Sir Leicester Dedlock had had reason to grumble of his troubles, surely they would have been fantiques to him. It is noteworthy that 'I don't think', so common a London catchword some years ago, is at least as old as Samuel Weller.

FINEER

OF the great 'Pam's' father and his lyrical knack Philip Guedalla wrote that 'Palmerston's pieces sounded very pretty to Mr. Walpole, although the snarling Tickell exclaimed a few years later that

> With chips of wit and mutilated lays
> Here Palmerston fineers his *bouts rhimées*'.

The embittered poet even hinted that the Viscount, who was now a member of the Board of Admiralty, 'like Ariel wrecked navies with a song'.

It is unusual nowadays to find the old form and spelling of veneer. Veneering was the application of thin strips of fine wood to the top of a heavy article and became an obvious metaphor for imposed decoration and surface glitter. The rough Scottish lad who, when congratulated on having had the advantage of upbringing and education in Aberdeen, added, 'Ay, but ah got ma po-lish in Dundee', could have said that he was fineered in the latter city. Veener has, inevitably for us, a touch of venom in it, though in fact there is no inherent suggestion of vice, much less of poison, in covering furniture with a finer surface. But veneer has a malicious tang to it and certainly Dickens's Mr. Veneering was set down in malice. There is scarcely a better chapter in the whole of Dickens, in my opinion, than that in *Our Mutual Friend* called 'A Piece of Work', concerning the way in which Mr. Hamilton Veneering, that 'very new and slightly sticky' man, is 'brought in' for Pocket-Breaches. Podsnap had said, 'You will infer that I don't care about Parliament from the fact of my not being there.' Veneering did care.

> Britannia, sitting meditating one fine day (perhaps in the attitude in which she is presented on the copper coinage), discovers all of a sudden that she wants Veneering in Parliament. It occurs to her that Veneering is a 'representative man' – which cannot in these times be doubted – and that Her Majesty's faithful Commons are incomplete without him. So Britannia mentions to a legal gentleman of her acquaintance that if Veneering will 'put down' five thousand pounds, he may write a couple of initial letters after his name at the extremely cheap rate of two thousand five hundred per letter. It is clearly understood between Britannia and the legal gentleman that nobody is to take up the five thousand pounds, but that being put down they will disappear by magical conjuration and enchantment.

Veneering spelt Fineering would not have been as good. But I like the form fineering for verses or for a prose style.

FINKLE

I HAVE been asked why finkle in the North of England means a small street or lane. In looking about for an answer I found an odd coincidence. Fynkle in Scottish means fennel; vennel in the North and in Scotland means a small street or lane. Has there been some confusion of f and v, so that the use of fynkle for fennel turned a vennel into a finkle? A small point, but interesting if true.

FLIRT

TO flirt was originally to strike or to knock. Then to scoff or jeer at somebody. Then to jerk. Birds flirt their wings and ladies, of old, would flirt their fans. Flirt, in the now commoner sense, of 'making love without serious intentions' or 'to trifle amorously', is as old as the eighteenth century. It could be used in dignified English. It then drifted downwards and almost below stairs and is now much rarer than it used to be. It seems to belong to the age of 'spooning', not that of 'making passes'. It was used by Ouida of her Guardees without any notion that flirting was a practice for the lower orders and not for such of the highest in the land as the Hon. Bertie Cecil, 'second son of Viscount Royallieu and known generally in the Brigades as Beauty'. Bertie kept a dancing-lady called Zu-Zu in the 'prettiest little box in the world' near Market Harborough where she attended the meet in a 'little toy-trap with its pair of snowy ponies'. The Hon. Bertie had a more official love. But, as Ouida put it

> Bertie would not have been the consummate tactician, the perfect flirt, the skilled and steeled campaigner in the boudoirs that he was, if he had not been equal to the delicate task of managing both the peeress and the ballet-dancer with inimitable ability, even when they placed him in the seemingly difficult dilemma of meeting them both with twenty yards between them on the neutral ground of the gathering of the Pytchley

> or the Tailby — a task he had achieved with victorious brilliance more than once already this season.

What seems odd to us now is that the ugly and vulgar little word *flirt* should once have been linked with such august phraseology as 'steeled campaigner in the boudoirs'.

FRISK

A FRISK for a day or night 'out' is Johnsonian English and we might renew the Doctor's taste in that regard.

> One night when Beauclerk and Langton had supped at a tavern in London, and sat till about three in the morning, it came into their heads to go and knock up Johnson, and see if they could prevail on him to join them in a ramble. They rapped violently at the door of his chambers in the Temple, till at last he appeared in his shirt, with his little black wig on the top of his head instead of a nightcap, and a poker in his hand, imagining, probably, that some ruffians were coming to attack him. When he discovered who they were, and was told their errand, he smiled, and with great good humour agreed to their proposal:
>
> 'What, is it you, you dogs! I'll have a *frisk* with you.'
>
> He was soon drest, and they sallied forth together into Covent-Garden, where the greengrocers and fruiterers were beginning to arrange their hampers, just come in from the country. Johnson made some attempts to help them; but the honest gardeners stared so at his figure and manner, and odd interference, that he soon saw his services were not relished. They then repaired to one of the neighbouring taverns, and made a bowl of that liquor called Bishop, which Johnson had always liked; while, in joyous contempt of sleep from which he had been roused, he repeated the festive lines:
>
> Short, O short then be thy reign,
> And give us to the world again!

After that they went rowing and prepared for a further day of frisking. But Langton remembered 'a date' for breakfast with some ladies. Johnson rebuked him for 'leaving his social friends to go and sit with a set of un-idea'd girls'.

This use of social is pleasant. We, with our social welfare and social reform, have made the adjective so solemn. Its eighteenth-century association was with talk and glasses. Un-idea'd hardly needs rescue. But it has the Doctor's vigour.

Johnson defined frisky as 'gay; airy; a low word'. I am told that in an 1818 edition of *Johnson's Dictionary*, revised by H. J. Todd, there is the word Friskal, defined by Todd as 'a leap; a caper', with a quotation from a Ben Jonson masque:

> Ixion, – turned dancer, does nothing but cut capreols, fetch friskals, and lead levaltoes with the Lamiae.

A capreol is a roebuck or a tendril. Presumably cutting capreols meant leaping like a roe or joining a saltatory stag-party. But not stags only. What of the hind let loose?

> Make haste, my beloved, and be thou like to a roe or a young hart upon the mountains of spices.

So ends the Song of Solomon – with a capreol note. So are two of the Wisest of Mankind, Solomon and Johnson, linked together with a friskal. And both, it seems, were good social fellows for a frisk.

Later, I was reading the reminiscences of an up-to-date burglar, who, after capture and conviction, explained his technique which had given him a year or two of luxurious liberty. After telling how he forced a window and entered a house, he said that he then 'frisked the rooms'. By this I presume that he meant turning out drawers and cupboards and throwing everything about in a hurried search for saleable stuff.

Then there is friskin for a young lively sprig. The Elizabethans used it of either sex. A lad's wench or friskin foots it in a lively dance (Nash) and Dekker has 'Sayst thou so, friskin?' in dramatic dialogue.

FRITINANCY

I OWE to a volume called *D.O.U.W.* (*Dictionary of Unusual Words*) a quotation from Eric Linklater's *Poet's Pub*,

> 'The most significant noise of earth is the singing of birds,' said the professor with determination.
>
> 'Fritinancy,' declared the young man beside the fire.
>
> 'What's that?' said the professor.
>
> 'I said fritinancy, which is the whimper of gnats and the buzzing of flies.'
>
> 'You're talking nonsense.'

Sir Thomas Browne has fritinience for twittering. The Linklater version of the word is even happier. Hamlet's 'Buzz, buzz' suggests that he too might have liked the term. His Osric was obviously a fritinancy boy and there is a plentiful fritinience in Rosencrantz and Guildenstern. The letters 'fri' appear to suit the mood and practice of tedious levity. For example, who is more naturally prone to fritinancy than some old frizzed fribble, out on a frisk and meeting a fringillaceous fricatrice who happens to be free and soon gets fried?

(Fringillaceous means finch-like, fried is modern for tipsy, and fricatrice is Jonson's frank label for a 'trull').

He frets her with the frills and frippery of small talk and fritters his time away with the frivolous company of his street-fritillary (butterfly). To which it may be replied that a friendly but frigid friar, of morals not easy friable, would, with the same initial letters, set a very different example. But, on the whole, the 'fri's' are light company. They may, at their worst, be lewd as well: in their most innocent and not least tiresome form, they are sure to be fritinant.

GALLIVANT

IS gallivanting gaily vaunting? Or is it some collision of gallantry and vanity? The authorities are agnostics here. I commented before on the rich assemblage of words beginning with 'gal', a fact itself, perhaps, symbolic of pleasant dalliance. You might even in these days gallivant, amid a galaxy of film-stars, to a gala performance, where amid the galimatias (babble of conversation) a galanty-show (or shadow-play) would be thrown on the screen. Does not gallivant sufficiently hint the splendours – if so you may deem them – of such an occasion? Later the galliards of the Company might dance a gallopade and sup off a galeeny (guinea-fowl) or gallinule (small hen) flavoured with galingale galore followed by a gallimaufry of sweets and washed down with Galician wine. Perhaps, if you were a poor stranger, admitted on sufferance to such high revels, you would on a winter night have to go padding home in galligaskins (leggings) and galoches (or goloshes). Or, with luck, you might end your gallivant by going galumphing home in somebody else's motor-car.

GIBBOUS

ONE is used to gibbous moons, i.e. to moons whose illuminated section is larger than a semi-circle. I was surprised to find the word applied to a deformed or hunch-backed lady. Shakespeare's son-in-law, Dr. John Hall – or rather the translator from Hall's Latin of his medical casebook called (simply and superbly) *Select Observations on English Bodies* – had this of one of his patients: 'Mistress Woodward, of Avon Dassett, a maid very witty and well bred, yet gibbous, aged 28.' It is less painful to be called gibbous than misshapen?

GLAUR

THE Scottish glaur is very nearly glamour and yet it means mud. I think it has crossed the Border southwards and well might stay with the English. I remember as a boy a hilarious Banffshire game-keeper who delighted to call on 'Wullie, Shon and Tam' to

> Brush the glaur frae off your kilts
> And come and hae a dram.

Glaury and clarty run together in the miry lexicon.

A correspondent writes to me:

> My mother, who was born in a small town in Galloway, and lived there as a girl until about 1890, used to be fond of quoting a certain old character of the town, who was notorious for never washing and justified this practice with the words, 'the clartier the cosier'.

He also wrote of an English schoolmaster teaching in Scotland. He hears a boy using the word glaur and asks its meaning. 'Drookit stour, a' coorse', was the answer. Drookit stour is drenched dust. Both words are, like glaur, fit for any poet's pen.

GLOAT

To gloat originally was to make a squinting amorous glance. One can imagine such a look on the face of the lecherous King Claudius of Denmark. Would not this bloat king be also a gloat king? Then, presumably, since the covetous one usually got what he wanted, the ugly word gloat was transferred to rejoicing in the achievement and the satisfaction. 'Fids, I gloat', cried Beetle. I am reminded by one of another academy that Winchester, when it speaks of gloating, uses the prettier word to junket. I referred previously to Horace Walpole's junkettaceous as an adjective applicable to hedonistic ladies. Perhaps the Wykehamist usage links with this. Gloat did well for the eye-work of lickerish fribbles. But it is too coarse for any decent satisfaction. To junket over a good round of golf or a hand of Bridge well played or even a pretty set of verses may be seemly: but to gloat can hardly be pleasant – or even tolerable.

GOBBLE

READING *The Golfer's Manual, by a Keen Hand* (1857) I found in its glossary some information as to the links lingo of the Mutiny year. If you rushed your put (one 't' in those days) at the hole and it fell in, then it was a gobble: if you ran down a long put contrary to expectation, it was a steal. Both terms are excellent. Why were they so widely abandoned? The term gobble reminds me of a golfer who said to me of putting, 'Holes are like fish. There are days when they just won't bite. Then comes a glorious occasion when they seem to rise up and gobble every time you push a ball at them.' I fancy that few of the Keen Hand's fellow-players admitted a 'steal' in their own putting. Only their opponents committed that kind of larceny.

GRAMERCY

NEW YORK has as good a place-name as any in London – and perhaps better than any – namely Gramercy Park. It may not be a Park, as we understand it, and the neighbourhood may not be quite up to the high and courteous suggestion of the earlier word. But there it is and to the person who does not know New York, Gramercy Park has a fairy-tale quality; here, one feels, the stricter sect of Puritan told tales from Grimm and Andersen to his children. The Puritan Milton used gramercy as a noun to signify special merit. A school-master of Milton's time, surveying his pupils' tasks and spying an 'alpha quality' paper, might have exclaimed 'What gramercy is this!' (No pun on grammar or Grammar School is intended.) 'God give you great thanks' was the Frenchified beginning of gramercy and so it became a general word of acclamation and gratitude. It turns up happily in the dialogue of the old drama and implies more courtesy than a mere 'thank'ee', while it makes more melody.

Gramercy has nothing to do with the old word, grame: it is, in fact, its very opposite. For grame was anger, vexation, and burning spite. It burned like a glead or ember. The heroes of the ballads could be fired with a glead of glame and for what they did then nobody would say 'gramercy'. Since I have wandered off among the coals of fire let me recount the queerest phrase I know for 'consumed with love'. It occurs in an Elizabethan translation of Ovid. Medea is telling Jason of her passion,

> Then saw I thee and perisht eke inflamed
> With fire unknowne, and fried with straungie gleade.

One has heard of lovers kindled, fired, scorched, and consumed. Fried, sometimes now slang for drunk, seems as little romantic to modern ears as any word could be.

GUMPTION

Do not tell me that Finance and Industry have no poetry. Consider this from a financial prospectus concerning 5 per cent Pref. Cum., etc. Were I an investor in the Company concerned, I would be an owner and vendor of 'Masticon, Gumption, and Multicore Solder'. 'Almost singing themselves they run.' Immediately and songfully I see the Company's chairman as

> A Masticon, Gumption, and Multicore Solderman,
> Member of Parliament, J.P. and Alderman.

What exactly is gumption, when it is not shrewdness, common-sense and the presence of gorm? Presumably there must be a quality of gorm, if stupid people can be gormless. (Vernon Bartlett wrote from some blue void in far-off seas to remind me that the Russian for stupid sounds like 'gloopy', which would be a perfect word, half loopy, half goofy, for our own lackers of gorm, nous, and gumption.) But let us return to Gumption, in this case (see Prospectus) a Smooth Paste Cleanser. But it is also (see Dictionary) the art of preparing colours. It is odd that a nation, not wildly aesthetic in taste, should have taken from the paint-box its synonym for sturdy common sense and for absence of 'gloopiness'.

ONE of the best of our comic columnists, in mocking the usual Spring Rites of the Children's Hour and Kiddies' Culture type, printed a talk with a Crocus, in which the latter kept repeating, 'I am the har-bin-ger of the Spring'. This made me wonder about a harbinger, who is usually the porter of news but not in the ordinary prose of today. Few of us would enter a room and remark, 'I am the harbinger of bad news. A man has just run out of the house with our hostess's mink-coat'. Harbing or Harbingering is 'period'.

The harbinger was originally a Billeting Officer. He went ahead of the medieval army, announced that the lads were on the way, and either hired or annexed the requisite accommodation for the milords, vassals, and serfs who were engaged in thumping across Merrie England while prosecuting the tedious, interminable business of the baronial wars. (Harbergage is the Middle English for a lodging and here we are in touch with harbouring in general and the French 'auberge'). Then, rather oddly, the harbinger's original job of finding bed-and-breakfast for the brutal and licentious soldiery was forgotten: he dwindled to a mere messenger. But the fair proportions of his name commended him to the poets and he was given new status as a courier and forerunner of all sorts of august arrivals, dawns, dames, and what you will. Aurora was a tigress for harbingers.

> For night's swift dragons cut the clouds full fast,
> And yonder shines Aurora's harbinger;
> At whose approach, ghosts, wandering here and there,
> Troop home to churchyards.

Thus Shakespeare's Puck on the coming of Dawn.

John Milton saw Delilah as a stately ship,

> With all her bravery on, each tackle trim,
> Sails fill'd, and streamers waving,
> Courted by all the winds that hold them play,
> An amber scent of odorous perfume
> Her harbinger.

(Forever Amber!)
Or – passing to less agreeable matters –

> Make all our trumpets speak; give them all breath,
> Those clamorous harbingers of blood and death.

So, with Macduff commanding, harbinger returns to his military duties.

HEADLE

SIDLE is often quoted as an interesting and useful back-formation from side-long. If to go side-long is to sidle, why, I am asked, should going head-long not be headling? Why not indeed? Headling for home suggests a good deal more of eagerness and energy than does heading for home. Back-formations such as burgle from burglar are fairly common and are certainly sensible. The comedians have tried to establish buttle from butler and for some reason they failed. Now that the butler, an expensive creature not likely to flourish among the fauna of our new social democracy, is disappearing, the verb to 'buttle', has less chance than ever. But people and things are undoubtedly headling in every direction, some towards bankruptcy and chaos, others towards supersonic speeds and the breaking of all records in size, noise, and nastiness. We are a generation of headlers rather than of sidlers and should be ready to employ so accurate a term.

ISABEL

ISABEL is a yellowish-brown colour. Nobody, as far as I can discover, knows why. Professor Weekley writes of isabel:

> inadequately defined by Brewer as 'the yellow of soiled calico', but easily recognized by anyone who has seen the 'isabelline bear' at the Zoo. The constantly repeated story is

that, during the siege of Ostend, the Archduchess Isabella swore not to change her chemise till the fortress fell. As the siege lasted from 1601 to 1604, this imperious lady endured some discomfort and made a new colour fashionable at her court. If we turn to the *Oxford Dictionary*, we find that, in 1600, Queen Elizabeth's wardrobe included, 'One rounde gowne of Isabelle-colour satten set with silver spangles'.

O.E.D., of course, also turns down the Archduchess, knowing that isabel appeared far too early on the colourman's list. Isabel has been applied to species of pigeon, peach, fish, and bear.

As a Christian name it is a variant of Elizabeth, a fact which seems more easily explicable if the old spelling of Esobel is kept in mind. A child in the nursery, attempting Elizabeth, might well say Esobel. Isabel was the French and Italian form of Elizabeth, which comes from the Hebrew Elisheba ('God has sworn'). No Christian name has had more variants and abbreviations: Bessy, Betsy, Bess, Lizzie, Liza, Lizbeth, Tetty, Beth, Elspeth, Ishbel, Elsie, Elsa, Lisa, Lisette, Betty, Bettina and even Babette are all attributed to the great Elize. Of course some of these are now used without reference to or knowledge of the Elizabethan source. Camden (1605) wrote that the Spaniards 'always translated Elizabeth into Isabel and the French into Isabeau'. In Wittycombe's *Oxford English Dictionary of Christian Names* Isabel is mentioned as being one of the commonest English girl's names in the Middle Ages. But this does not explain why Isabelline birds, bears, fruits, fishes, etc. are yellow-brown and sand-coloured. Was there another unwashed, unlaundered Isabel long before the Archduchess, whose claim to a doubtful honour is now so vigorously pushed aside?

JEJUNE

A MOST effective word for empty, thin, barren, or desiccated. It was a favourite of that gracious figure, J. L. Strachan-Davidson, who was Master of Balliol when I was 'in statu pup'. He did not disdain to take Freshmen's essays, despite the majesty of his office; and most charmingly did he assess and dismiss them. I remember one young man, who held his own prose in considerable esteem, being thus addressed by the Master. Strachan-Davidson had a curious habit of drawing out the 'ur' in his hesitant speech and giving the 'u' a foreign richness. His comment, after the essay, so sedulously attempting brilliance, had been read to him, ran thus,

> U-u-r, Mr. Blank, you have, u-u-r, a spark of style, a spark of style, but your matter is, u-u-r, deplorably, u-u-r, jee-june!

This last was on a high, piping note with the 'jee' prolonged. The adjective Jejune came in with memorable point and melody. It terminated the judgment to perfection.

JOWL

JOWL we know for its proximity to cheek. Cheek by jowl, cheek by jawbone. It also means the fat of the neck or dewlap. I like it especially as a verb. It is a grand term for beat or bang. Yorkshire dialect claims it with such reference as this:

> 'Th' poleece seized 'em and jowled their heeads together,

but it was a national not a local word for centuries back. The Clown in *All's Well That Ends Well*, arguing to the text 'If I be his cuckold, he's my drudge', maintains that infidelity makes all men one.

> If men could be contented to be what they are, there were no fear in marriage; for young Charbon the puritan and old Poysam the papist, howsome'er their hearts are sever'd in religion, their heads are both one – they may jowl horns together, like any deer i' the herd.

We should have kept jowl. And punce too. Punce is a more expressive word than punch for the same thing, especially if pronounced with the 'u' long. It is, I think, more Lancastrian than Yorkist. The afore-mentioned 'poleece' I visualize as having punced their roughs before they started on the jowling process.

LADS AND LASSES

'M.E. LADDE. Of unkn. etym.' So it is a mystery, this most-common of our little greeting and descriptive words. Originally it meant a young servant or lackey: then it came up in the world to be a kindly, almost affectionate term, especially in Scotland where the inevitable -ie attached itself and made the braw, bonnie laddie. Shakespeare's 'golden lads' are contrasted with chimney-sweepers, lads having then become considerable persons. The history of lass was similar. 'M.E. lasce.' First she was a serving wench and then even Cleopatra herself could be a 'lass unparalleled'.

Nowadays the use of the word 'lad' in poetry immediately sets one thinking of Housman. Stewart Perowne, having exchanged the waters of Babylon for those of the Spanish Main, sent me as a Christmas card a piece from a crowded ship, Barbados-bound, entitled 'Baghdad Remembered in Winter'. With his permission I quote:

Red with the blood of Abel,
  The guilty river flees
Avenging ghosts of Babel,
  Beneath the tattered trees
  That lean along the leas.

Mute now are music's daughters,
  Now broken summer's toys;
No longer willowed waters
  Re-echo little joys
  Of happy girls and boys.

New springs will start to meet you
  And lads will laugh again;
New moons will soft entreat you,
  And purge the waters' stain –
  But not the curse of Cain.

This, he adds, was prepared according to his own recipe, which contains: 'Guilt, Biblical allusion, hopelessness, alliteration, lads, and a noun twisted into an epithet, a recipe which is guaranteed to produce instant relief in cases of even the most acute Housmania.'

The habit of writing Housmanics had begun long before A. E. H. set to work. One of the early masters in this line was, surprisingly, the Grand Cham himself. How many would, without previous warning, sign these lines with the name of Samuel Johnson?

'Wealth, my lad, was made to wander,
  Let it wander as it will;
Call the jockey, call the pander,
  Bid them come and take their fill.

But, Johnson's they are, lad and all. No doubt Housman did overplay the lads, lightfoot or grave-yard-minded, and so made the use of the word in a lyric almost a guarantee of some Salopian melancholy in the air. I have wondered why Shakespeare wrote:

Golden lads and girls all must
Like chimney-sweepers come to dust

when he might have made it 'Golden lads and lasses must'. Was the association of lads and lasses already trite to him? Certainly the surprise of finding girl after lad is effective with us nowadays, when girl continually meets boy, but not so often, except in Housmanics, meets lad.

Emily Dickinson united the sexes thus in her 'Cemetery Song':

This quiet dust was Gentlemen and Ladies,
  And Lads and Girls;
Was laughter and ability and sighing,
  And frocks and curls.

This passive place a Summer's nimble mansion
Where Bloom and Bees
Fulfilled their Oriental Circuit,
Then ceased like these.

I wonder why she did not write 'Boys and Girls'. She was under no compulsion of rhyme, wherein the lad, capable of being sad, mad, or glad, scores over the boy who may give joy but would hate to be coy.

LAIR

THE English have a good vocabulary of burial. Grave, sepulchre, and tomb could hardly be bettered for those who wish, or are compelled, to toll the mourning bell. The sharp sting of death is in the brevity of grave and tomb, its ponderous finality is in the weight of sepulchre. The faithful who believe in a bodily resurrection may expect graves to open, hardly sepulchres. The latter has such an imprisoning sound. The Scots have kept the old English lair for a burying-place and, seen in cold print, the word has a shiversome ferocity. This appeared in *The Times* early in 1947:

PUBLIC NOTICES

CHURCH OF ST. JOHN THE EVANGELIST

EDINBURGH

Notice is given to all OWNERS OF LAIRS in the BURYING GROUND of the above Church that it is proposed to turf this Burying Ground, removing all curbstones, railings, etc., between individual lairs. Lair-holders will not be asked to contribute to the cost of this work. Circulars have been sent to all known lair-holders, but interested parties who have not received a circular are requested to communicate with the undersigned not later than Friday, 31st January, 1947.

MAURICE N. DURLAC, W.S. Secretary to the Vestry.
4, Charlotte Square, Edinburgh, 2. 17th January 1947.

The beasts of the fields go to their lairs and so, in Scotland still, can we. 'The grave's a fine and silent place' and so should a lair be too. It has a dark, untroubled suggestion. The word was used as a verb by Robert Fergusson, who sang so racily of the Edinburgh which Burns was soon to conquer, owing much to Fergusson's happy new use of the old vernacular in traditional Scottish rhythms. Fergusson died at the age of twenty-four, in a mania of religious melancholy which seems wholly out of keeping with the pagan jollity of his social scene as he described it in the Scottish capital or at Leith Races. He was laired in the Canongate burying ground and Burns placed a stone upon his grave. In his poem on Auld Reekie he had denounced civic dignitaries thus:

> For POLITICS are a' their mark,
> Bribes latent, and corruption dark:
> If they can eithly turn the pence,
> Wi' city's good they will dispense;
> Nor care tho' a' her sons were lair'd
> Ten fathom i' the auld kirk-yard.

The friend who sent me the cutting from *The Times*, added that the Tudor and Jacobean men, with their rich, musty lingo and images for all the cerements and vaults of death, should have retained lair and not passed it over the Border. He mentioned Webster in particular and I agree. For one who writes of man, 'Thou ar't a box of worm-seede, at best', there should be lairs awaiting the sowing of so macabre a seed.

LAMPOON

THE double 'o' is always striking. In this case the old French 'lampon', a drinking song and presumably not always a polite one, was lengthened to become the lampoon or satirical attack in words without music. In a similar, queer way carton, a piece of stout paper on which designs were first roughed out, became cartoon, a word now restricted to the use of paper for a mordant and satirical drawing. Lampoons and cartoons are two weapons in the same armoury, whose walls, perhaps, the latter may festoon. Their natural victims are poltroons and, in some cases, pantaloons. Ireland throws in its gossoons, Nature its baboons. People ending in -oon appear to be asking for contemptuous dismissal: they receive their punishment with two more blows from the same 'oonish' implement, being caricatured in cartoon and lampooned in stinging verses.

LONGINQUIPETITE

DANIEL GEORGE, delving into D'Urfey's *The Campaigners*, found this in the Preface and sent it on for analysis and, I fancy, for admiration too.

> . . . the Reformer (Collier) who, for all the gravity in some part of his Book, and the solid Piety he would insinuate into his Arguments, I perceive to be a Joker, and as full of Puns, Conundrums, Quibbles, Longinquipetites, and Tipiti-witchets, as the rest of us mortals.

This is Mr. Polly's 'sesquippledan verboojuice' indeed. I take the longinquipetite to be a distantly sought or, as we say, far-fetched allusion or erudite play upon words. Tipiti-witchet is what? Perhaps it is the hangover from Tudor Euphuism with its elaborate patterning, prinking, and balancing of words. Conundrum, which D'Urfey includes with his longinquipetites, is an odd word whose origin defies the lexicographers. It began life as a person, one who grumbles and quibbles, a crotchet-monger; then it became the quibble itself, the tricky play on words, and finally a tricky question, a puzzle. The Elizabethans used a conundrum as they also used a maggot. To have a maggot on your brain was to entertain whimsies and crotchets. Maggots thus became synonymous with queer and troublesome fancies. The tipiti-witchets of D'Urfey's vocabulary are obviously happier quips and quirks than are the maggots in the Tudor mind. Shakespeare used maggot as an adjective for ostentation. It occurs in *Love's Labour's Lost*, a play in which, speaking through the lips of Berowne, he indulges in, repents of, and finally disclaims the whole breed of taffeta phrases in which would certainly be included longinquipetites and tipiti-witchets.

MANAVILINS

SURELY we need manavilins today. For these are odds and ends, 'supplementaries to the ordinary fare'! Points goods, as the grocer would say in our time. I must have come across manavilins in my childhood, for I read *Robbery Under Arms*, by Rolf Boldrewood, with a good appetite for more and it is in Boldrewood's text that Dr. Thomas Wood, as a new editor thereof, met this rare word for rare-bits, Australian rather than Welsh. It was carried to Australia, presumably, by sailors who had used the verb manarvel for pilfering small stores.

Manarvel is a term of genuine size and dignity for a small shabby matter and might be better appended to malfeasance on the grand scale. 'Convicted of manarvelling to the extent of two million pounds, a City Financier was yesterday sentenced . . .' Manarvel, on the other hand, would be a good, imposing, well-sounding name for a Money Baron. To me it suggests solid worth rather than light fingers. Might we not all feel more secure if the Chairman of the Company, in whose ordinary stock we made a mild investment, were called Lord Manarvel? Perhaps, but only if we were not students of the larger dictionaries and of the lexicons of sailors' slang. For then we should find the fellow out. Manavelins or manavelings was also a term for small cash left over after the accounts had been made up. It occurs to me that composing word-books of this kind might be called a dabbling in the manavilins of language. Or why not a verb, similar to but not identical in meaning with manarvel? To go manaviling would then be to browse over books in order to pick one's flowers, whether they be whole poems and passages of prose or single words.

Batty Langley, who wrote on *New Principles of Gardening* and advised on the laying out of Labyrinths and Wildernesses in the year 1728, included Serpentine Meanders among the pleasures of a well-planned estate. Here is Langley's catalogue of pleasures and pleasaunces aimed at fulfilling his (surely difficult) injunction that 'all Gardens be grand, beautiful, and natural'.

> That the several Parts of a beautiful Rural Garden, are Walks, Slopes, Borders, Open Plains, Plain Parterres, Avenues, Groves, Wildernesses, Labyrinths, Fruit-Gardens, Flower-Gardens, Vineyards, Hop-Gardens, Nurseries, Coppiced Quarters, Green Openings, like Meadows; Small Inclosures of Corn, Cones of Evergreens, of Flowering Shrubs, of Fruit Trees, of Forest-Trees, and mix'd together: Mounts, Terraces, Winding Valleys, Dales, Purling Streams, Basons, Canals, Fountains, Cascades, Grottos, Rocks, Ruins, Serpentine Meanders, Rude Coppices, Hay-Stacks, Wood-Piles, Rabbit and Hare-Warrens, Cold Baths, Aviaries, Cabinets, Statues, Obelisks, Manazeries, Pheasant and Partridge-Grounds, Orangeries, Melon-Grounds, Kitchen-Gardens, Physick or Herb-Garden, Orchard, Bowling Green, Dials, Precipices, Amphitheatres, etc.

Nothing 'natural' about all that. But much that takes the ear as well as the eye.

By the time a milord had arranged for all these fine-sounding items his bill, even in those days, would have been considerable. Manazerie is an odd spelling of menagerie, which, originally applied to a cattle-farm, came in the eighteenth century to be used of captive animals on show.

Meander, as most people know, was a winding river in Phrygia, whose mazy course turned it, by way of Greek, into an English verb and, less commonly, an English noun. It would scarcely have lived on, I think, if the sound of it had not so well suggested a vagrant curvature of motion.

Sweet Echo, sweetest nymph, that liv'st unseen
Within thy airy shell
By slow Meander's margent green
And in the violet-embroidered dell.

This song in *Comus* shows clearly why Meander survived. It has the quietitude as well as the vagabond nature of some oozy and wandering stream. A mountain torrent can take furious turns, but it does not meander, at least for me. Coleridge's heavily alliterative line,

Five miles meandering with a mazy motion,

seems far more apposite to our native Thames or any of our quiet Avons than to his sacred and sometimes violent Alph, which

sank in tumult to a lifeless ocean.

I cannot associate tumult with meander, whose name discounts the plash of rapids or the roar of falls.

Macaulay's review of Robert Montgomery's poems quotes:

The soul aspiring pants its source to mount,
As streams meander level with their fount.

It was easy to add that streams do nothing of the sort: they would not get far if they did.

MECCA AND MECKERING

When a friend told me that he was going Meckering round Scotland I was naturally puzzled. Then he explained that he was doing a species of High Temple or G.H.Q. Tour, including all the Meccas, St. Andrews (golf), Loch Leven (trout), Deeside (salmon), Loch Ness (monsters), Glencoe (massacres), Glen Shiel (Bonnie Prince Charlie) and then, lest letters be neglected, back by way of Ayrshire (Burns) and Abbotsford (Scott). I mentioned that he should call it Mecca-ing, not Meckering, but he said that nobody would be so precise. I also said that he was omitting the finest, most exciting city in Great Britain, Edinburgh. He asked me how one Meckerized there? Who was its Allah? I could only reply that in Edinburgh one saluted, as nowhere else in this country and perhaps in the world, two sides of the human genius, romantic to the south of Prince's Street and classical to the north of it. Edinburgh is the Mecca of all with eyes in their heads and that capacity for wonder without which life merely flows lack-lustre to the grave.

Mecca, the holy city of the Moslems, had, according to the omniscience of the *Oxford English Dictionary*, worked its way into our language as a synonym for temple or headquarters by 1850. Since then it has remained a conquering cliché.

Presumably we have chosen the word Mecca because our own faith's holy cities are too holy to be suitable. Would it be quite nice to call St. Andrews the Jerusalem of Golfers or Newmarket the Rome of the Racing Fraternity? Art and Culture are the great Mecca-makers. Obviously the first of our English Meccas is Stratford-upon-Avon. The Birthday of the Bard is in fact unknown, but it is generally guessed to be April 23rd, which happens to be also the anniversary of his death fifty-two years later and St. George's Day too. So here is an outsize in anniversaries and it is properly honoured with Meckering on the grand scale, complete with bunting, lunching, speeches, processions, gala performances and a Financial Statement by the Governors of the Shakespeare Memorial Theatre. This was, at one time, very satisfactory.

One would have expected the Scots to do much more with the Burns Industry than they have managed so far. Scots assert their loyalty to the Immortal Memory with great gusto (and with what libations can nowadays be managed) once a year (January 25th), but the Mecca side of the cult has been hampered by multiplicity of shrines. Burns was born at Alloway (see Cottage and Monument), married at Mauchline (see Poosy Nancy's Tavern and National Memorial with Tower) and drank in Ayr (see Tam o' Shanter Inn and Auld Brig). But Meccas should, for convenience, be compact. That is where Stratford gains.

The City of London seems to be nobody's Mecca and no solemn

anniversary processions in honour of Gresham of Gresham's Law are allowed to hold up business in Threadneedle Street. Sir Richard Whittington, who gratified Henry V by not insisting on having loans repaid, was a model Success Type, showing all the Boys' Club Virtues, Courage, Perseverance, Initiative, Kindness to Animals, etc., and there is a Whittington Stone on Highgate Hill. But I have never seen a covey of Success Addicts dancing round it on Richard's birthday.

Statesmen, too, rarely create a Mecca. Has anyone ever heard of a wild scamper to Disraeli's Hughenden on Primrose Day or a nation-wide Liberal call to Hawarden for Gladstonian goings-on? The Russians have done some Mecca-work with Lenin's tomb in Moscow, but it is an astonishing fact that the great architect of Communism, Karl Marx, lies buried in Highgate Cemetery – in the heart of the Whittington country – in a narrow grave, which he shares with his wife, Jenny, a German who had Scottish blood in her, with his grandson, and with a Miss Delmuth, whom I take to have been a relative or companion-help.

A few of the faithful occasionally scatter red flowers upon this humble resting-place, which lies among the far more grandiose tombs of the London merchants. I once asked the attendant at the South Gate of Highgate Cemetery how to find the Marxian 'lair', in this labyrinth. He gave me the necessary 'rights and lefts' among the pathways and then added, 'Look for name of Scrimmage. Then behind that. No standing-up stone. Nothing showy. It's a flat job.' And there it is behind the big Scrymgeour stone – a 'flat job' – and so small. Certainly no Mecca. Yet the man below it gave our world a heave, and that by writing a book which not one in a thousand of his followers has ever read through and very few have even begun to attack. Perhaps, if he had made it easier, there would be a Marx Mecca at Highgate.

Royalty, of course, is a prolific source of Meckering. In 1945, to celebrate a tragic bicentenary, that of the ill-fated 'Forty-Five', there was an august concourse of Highlanders, some with birth-qualifications, others with only intellectual or emotional attachments, at Prince Charlie's towering monument on Loch Shiel, where the clans once gathered for the rising. Prince Charlie had very little Scottish blood in him: his mother was a Pole and his royal line was full of French and Italian ancestors. But Glen Shiel is still a Mecca for sentimental admirers of the Stuarts. Might we speak of Clan McMecker?

Bonnie Charlie was no Scot (his mother called him Carlo Mio) and the Brontës were no Yorkshire folk. Their original name was Prunty or Brunty. The father came from Ulster and the mother from Cornwall and the name Brontë, which is Greek for thunder and was the name of a foreign dukedom held by Admiral Nelson, was chosen by the Rev. Patrick for romantic reasons. But the Meckering in this case goes with the scene of the books. The region moors are real moors and usually the weather is 'wuthering'. The vicarage at Haworth is well kept. As at Stratford or Glen Shiel you may really get the feel of history walking. There are ghosts about and they may even grab you by the heart-strings. For that, surely, does Meckering exist.

MENALTY

THE menalty are the people of the Mean, now by no means a golden Mean, the mid-way class. They include the brain-workers or clerisy, to give them another old name still in use. In Hall's *Chronicles* they are the third estate, separating the Nobilitie and the Commonaltie. I have no objection to being called Middle Class, although the words are often used in a slightly depreciative way. Far from it. Indeed I am proud to belong to this immensely productive and inventive section of the community, which is usually and wrongly supposed to be only dull and stodgy. To call it, in Britain, the bourgeoisie is silly, since the British Middle Class has native characteristics. Clerisy is too suggestive of a single branch of our professional life and almost wears its dog-collar. To romanticize our Middle Class as a Menalty will do no injustice to the facts. But the word seems to be almost extinct. From death to life we might it yet recover.

MISBELIEVE

As a noun of assembly, obviously useful. Daniel George sent me a medieval list of Carving-terms (period of Henry VI) which reminds one how much the kitchens of that epoch depended on the fowler. But why the precisians of the pantry insisted on a new knife-word for capon, mallard, heron, crane, goose, swan, peacock, curlew, pheasant, quail, rail, plover, pigeon, and 'al smalle berdys' I cannot think. This form of verbal extravagance apparently gave great satisfaction. The carver 'disfigured' a peacock. It is a term applicable to the carving of many, whatever their victim. Since our rationing began, the male 'disfigurers' have mainly been deposed by careful wives who regard, no doubt justly, masculine sword-play at the dinner-table as wickedly wasteful or at least over-generous. The medieval frushing of birds, the displaying, dismembering, disfiguring, unlacing, unbracing, and all the rest of it, came from an overflowing larder. The man with the knife had no need to think of 'eightpennyworth of carcase meat' as we must do, with our poverty on one side and the hideous vocabulary invented by the Ministry of Food on the other. What, pray, was your 'intake of carcase-meat' last week?

But what has all this to do with misbelieve? Nothing, except that the list of carving-terms is followed by some jocose nouns of assembly in addition to the familiar 'Byldyng of rokes (rooks), murmuration of stares (starlings)' and so on. This list includes a 'nonpaciens of wyves' and a 'misbeleve of paynters'. That housewives should be thrawn, as the Scots say, is natural in hard times. (What a wonderful word is 'thrawn-gabbit', i.e. twisty-mouthed, sour, and peevish. 'A testy of wives' would not be a bad term of this order.) But why were 'paynters' mentioned as the most untrustworthy of men? Other artists have told far bigger lies. But a 'misbelieve' should be retained. As a journalist (and proud of it) I hesitate to suggest 'a misbelieve of reporters' or even of 'columnists'. But would a Misbelieve of Ministers be an unfair description of a Cabinet?

MOON-GLADE

GLADE or gleed was originally bright and the glad eye, a lively phrase now antiquated and almost extinct, happens to be as old as Chaucer.

So young, so lusty, with her eyen glade.

Therefore a glade was a light, bright place. Where the woods parted (or were cut down) there was admission for the bright thing, the light. The result was a glade. You could even have a glade of water in winter, between the frozen patches, though such water would hardly be brighter than ice.

Nicest use of all is moon-glade, which means the track of moonlight that bestrides the sea upon a shiny night. The word suggests a calm and shimmering beauty, with sea-scape and lunar radiance mingled to a gently plashing nocturne: moreover the word is music itself.

Glade was diminished when it sank to glad. Glade tidings have more splendour and nobility than glad ones and the 'glade eyen' of Chaucer sparkle with a happier lustre than did the glad ones of 1912 which was, I think, the peak-year for that phrase.

I would like to see moon-glade more employed in the word-picturing of nights at sea or beside the shore. The most charming moon-glades of my acquaintance were seen from pier-heads with the human illuminations, 'glade' enough in their own way, tranquilly outshone by the majesty of Nature.

MOUSE

WOMEN are said to be afraid of mice, regarding them as odious clamberers, no less pestilent than a daddy-longlegs, and even worse because they attack darkly from below instead of from above. Yet men have often thought mouse to be a term of high compliment and for centuries the loved-one was alluded to as mouse. Professor Leslie Hotson, explaining Mercutio's cryptic remark to Romeo,

'Dun's the mouse! The constable's own word', has shown that Dun here is punning on Romeo's last words 'I am done' and refers to the good Brown (Dun) Horse, the faithful servant. Dun had become (and long remained) a symbol for the less than glamorous but more than serviceable article or creature. So Dun's the mouse was a catch-phrase of the time for 'the quiet fellow's best' or some sentiment of that kind, mouse being the equivalent of darling.

Hotson has tracked down references to Dun as the mouse (or darling) in a number of 'Jacobethan' plays. 'The constable's own word' meant honest assurance, the Elizabethan constable being himself a well-intending amateur not showily dressed, the plain, honest-to-goodness citizen. Mouse as a term of endearment is common in Restoration Drama. Nowadays we prefer to name our pretty and dear ones after fruit, flowers, and sweetmeats. The Western World vows its affection to Honey and Peach and Candy. Our ancestors looked to the smaller animals and fishes for symbols of feminine enchantment. In a previous volume I quoted, on the nature of Moppet, a line from Puttenham's *English Poesie*, 'understanding by this word a little prety lady or tender, young thing, for so we call fishes'. We, who have turned the pretty, nimble trout into a term of contempt, especially if prefixed by 'old', pay scant regard to fish and are impolite to the mouse. 'A mousy little creature' is hardly a complimentary phrase. Yet to Shakespeare and his fellows, as we are reminded by the learned Leslie Hotson, mouse means darling, jewel, or, more modernly, 'the tops'.

NECESSARIES

No fictional detective, bidden to the scene of the crime, proceeded to his garage or (of old) his railway terminus without 'throwing a few necessaries into a bag'. Necessaries are never put in bags: they always appear to be hurled there with some violence. The usage of the word is old. Among those who have tossed their night-shift, as Highlanders the caber, was Hamlet's Laertes. Bidding goodbye to his father and sister, he said, 'My necessaries are embark'd: farewell'.

When did the tooth-brush join the roll of necessaries? It arrived in English Literature in 1690. But that does not mean that Romeo's Apothecary did not keep a dentifrice or two among his stuff'd alligator and 'old cakes of roses'.

What exactly constitutes a necessary is, of course, undecided. A Victorian climber in the Lake District, James Payn, adventured himself on the conquest of Fairfield, one of the Helvellyn group. Nowadays a youngster would be up and back in an afternoon, sustained only by a cheese-sandwich and a bun. But Payn, whose account I derive from G. S. Sandilands' *Anthology of the Lake District*, took the matter seriously, as indeed did all pedestrians assaulting the 'horrid hills' in those days.

> These were the chief of the necessaries which my sagacity procured for our night-bivouac and tremendous ascent: thirty-six bottles of bitter beer, two bottles of gin, two bottles of sherry, one gallon of water; four loaves of bread, one leg of lamb, one leg of mutton, two fowls, one tongue, half-pound of cigars, four carriage-lamps, and two packs of playing cards. We had also a large tent, which was carried upon the back of a horse. Three men were necessary to pitch this tabernacle and to carry the provisions. About five o'clock in the afternoon we started for the mountains with a huge train of admirers, forming the largest cavalcade that had ever left Ambleside before.

The climb began successfully. Signals were sent back to Ambleside and salvos of victory were discharged from a fowling-piece. But the rest was not so good. Indeed the bivouac was disastrous. A wind blew down the tent.

> In an instant, an unknown force hurled me from my kneeling posture, prostrate upon the ground, and some monster at the same moment seemed to leap upon me with inconceivable violence. The whole party experienced a sensation precisely similar. The last storm-puff had carried our tent clean off its pegs. For some minutes we were inextricably involved amidst guides, bottles, friends, cards, carriage lamps and cold meats,

besides finding a difficulty in breathing. I struggled as violently as any . . . and was the first to find myself ankle deep in the coldest water. . . .

Then came mist and rain. They returned, as drenched as otters, to be offered in Rydal the comfort of umbrellas. So perhaps the gin and sherry had not been unjustly called 'necessaries which my sagacity procured'. But one wishes, in these years, that the Ministry of Food would and could take a larger view of what necessity commands in larders or in knapsacks.

ORIENT

'THE corn was orient and immortal wheat which never should be reaped nor was ever sown. I had thought it stood from everlasting to everlasting.' Traherne's visionary harvest has become familiar by quotation, but how many of those who know the passage could exactly define 'orient wheat'? Orient literally means rising and might refer to a young crop, but it is nearly always applied to the rising sun and thence to the source of that spectacle, the Eastern horizon: thence came its application to Eastern lands. Orient can also mean the dawn itself. But since the dawn is bright and lustrous, orient came later to be an adjective of colour. Traherne's wheat might have been richly golden, like the surging sun. In any case, the roll of sound in the word is effective and drums its way finely in Francis Thompson's Orient Ode:

> Lo, in the sanctuaried East
> Day, a dedicated priest,
> In all his roles pontifical exprest,
> Lifteth slowly, lifteth sweetly,
> From out its Orient tabernacle drawn,
> Yon orbed sacrament confest
> Which sprinkles benediction through the dawn.

Orient as a verb has had a dismal fate and has become the tool of every tedious political writer who has to call a trend of opinion an 'ideological orientation'. Orientation begins as the placing of articles to face east, becomes transference eastward, facing eastward, and then the knowing of one's own position relative to the east. Finally the east drops out of it altogether and orientation becomes any kind of adjustment or position. The word has now been dreadfully overworked, especially by intellectuals, and I instinctively flinch when I see a sentence with orientation in it. Here, I know, is one of those gas-bag writers who wrap their politics in yards of verbal cotton-wool. 'Mr. Blank's political orientation is insufficiently integrated with realities and is based upon a geopolitical misconception about Russia's legitimate sphere of economic penetration.' Here, by the way, is a nice piece of English which has come to my desk. It is the first sentence of a 'Manifest of the F.I.A.L.S. in favour of militant peace.'

> Having noticed that between the two world wars, torrents of saliva and mountains of pamphlets have been used in vain to keep people from cutting one another's throats, we have come to the conclusion without being too presumptuous, that the combat against bellicism should be oriented towards new ideas of action.

F.I.A.L.S., which stands for Fédération Internationale des Arts, des Lettres, and des Sciences, later on puts its anti-bellicist trust in 'the U.N.E.S.C.O.', which shows considerable courage on the Federation's part. I thank it meanwhile for its resolve to spare us more 'torrents of saliva' and to get on with its unpresumptuous orientation.

ORT

At a time when the learned have to do their own washing-up, with little or no relief of scullions and of the maid that 'does the meanest chares', I am surprised that they should not keep in usage the brief, dismissive Shakespearean word 'ort'. The orts were scraps of food left over, the raw material of soup for humans and of swill for pigs, probably nowadays the substratum of those 'Viennese Steaks' that so libel the city of Vienna by their villainous composition. Shakespearean beggars craved for orts and ort became a metaphor for the fragmentary relics of anything, even of love itself. Cried Troilus in his despair,

> The fractions of her faith, orts of her love,
> The fragments, scraps, the bits, and greasy relics
> Of her oft-eaten faith, are bound to Diomed.

That is careless writing from a master-hand, with fragments following so close on fractions and with faith used twice in three lines, but, in its hatred of mess and grease it is truly Shakespearean, for William was fastidious. He particularly disliked the fawning of dogs round a table in order to pick up bits of candy or the orts of broken meat. They symbolized the flatterers and the 'seemers', as they are called in *Measure for Measure*.

Orts were removed, if not by the fawning spaniels and greyhounds, then by the scullions of the scullery. The Latin *scutella*, a dish, has given us the scullery where the dishes were kept and cleaned. Hence the base scullions of Elizabethan abuse. Falstaff called Hostess Quickly a scullion, rampallion, and fustilarian: the two latter are formidable missiles to discharge at any lady who is merely presenting her bill in the common routine of her catering business. A fustilarian is defined by *O.E.D.* as being, possibly, a comic formation based on fustilugs, and fustiluggery itself refers to fat and frowsiness, usually feminine. Fustilug or fustilarian certainly merits rediscovery and retention for application to a gross virago. We have travelled somewhat from the stale gravy and bits of fat and gristle of the ort-laden plate with which we began. I shall always associate orts with examinations done in a College Hall, since meals as well as questions are served up there and the former may affect the atmosphere quite as much as do the academic suggestions of the architecture and the high dignity of the portraits on the wall. One settled to do one's commenting or composing with a powerful reminder of orts beyond the screen or below stairs.

OUTRAGEOUS

I LIKE to find outrageous in its original sense of raging outwards. Trent, as North Midlanders still discover to their cost, is a river much given to flooding, and Defoe, whom a Grecian scholar might call a Potamophobe, a dreader of rivers, termed it 'a most outrageous stream'. Arnold Palmer, in his admirable notes to *Recording Britain*, has given more instances of this fear of fluvial 'outrage'. The tumbling Tees, which so decoratively parts Yorkshire and Durham, Defoe called 'terrible' and of the Derbyshire Derwent he wrote: 'That Fury of a River . . . we kept our Distance the Waters being out, for the Derwent is a frightful Creature when the Hills load her Current with Water: I say, we kept our Distance.' Potamophobia indeed!

What exactly did Hamlet mean by 'outrageous fortune'? A fortune, I suppose, that works outward, beyond due limit, like a fury of a river, a frightful creature. The trouble is that while Defoe's precept of judicious distance-keeping is practicable with most rivers, unless you have been silly enough to build a bungalow on easily submersible land, destiny is not so easily dodged or 'blanched'. We have got the word outrageous twisted round by now. For example, an outrageous schoolmaster should really be a choleric dominie much given to overflow of censure or of sarcasm. But the phrase would probably now be taken to mean a very bad, incompetent schoolmaster. If we say that some cricketer gave an outrageous display, do we mean that he became a Fury and made it prudent policy for the other side to mimic the potamophobe and, Defoe-like, keep their distance? No, such a term now generally describes a poor, incompetent display.

Shakespeare had not really made up his mind about outrage. Sometimes he used it of crime and assault, sometimes of overflowing emotion. His Valentine in *Two Gentlemen of Verona* agreed to live with the outlaws in the forest.

> Provided that you do no outrages
> On silly women or poor passengers

(Who would, at sight, attribute these lines to W.S.?)

In reply to this the Third Outlaw pledged detestation of 'such vile, base practices'. But Prince Escalus in *Romeo and Juliet* would cry,

> Seal up the mouth of outrage for awhile.

It is strange that Shakespeare never wrote of outrageous rivers because, as Dr. Caroline Spurgeon has pointed out in *Shakespeare's Imagery*, Avonian Will had seen a deal of flooded land in his boyhood and so had something of the Potamophobe inside him. Of his fifty-nine river images, observes this indefatigable statistician of metaphor, twenty-six are of different aspects of a river in flood. His floods are impatient and overbearing, angry, vexed, swollen, symbolic of the passion of ambitious, power-hungry, power-seizing men. Anybody who saw Stratford-amid-Avon after the great thaw of the great snows in the early spring of 1947 will appreciate both Shakespeare's potamophobia and Defoe's nervous retreat from outrageous waters, i.e. waters actually raging outwards.

PARAMOUNT

PAR for us generally signifies equality and the steady level. 'Par' at golf is level with the best. Financial stock may stand at par: if our investment sinks, we feel 'below par'. Paramount, at first sight, should therefore mean 'of equal quantity'. But, in fact, it is just the opposite and implies complete supremacy. The word rolls nicely on the tongue and between the lips. Its origin has more to do with mountain-tops than with amounts and it was early in favour for the summit, the sovereign, or, as they say now, the big shot and the ace. How well it rides in Wordsworth's lament for the emptiness of revolutionary France!

> No single volume paramount, no code,
> No master-spirit, no determined road,
> But equally a want of books and men.

This is a trifle hard on Bonaparte, whose paramountcy — as well as his code – could not fairly be overlooked. Wordsworth was well aware that the sound of paramount could be of great help to a line.

> The head and mighty paramount of truth,
> Immortal life, in never-fading worlds.

The anapaest, Greek name for two short syllables followed by a long one, is always an effective metrical foot, especially when the poet is seeking to express some rollicking, bellicose, or cavalcade mood.

> The Assyrian came down like a wolf on the fold
> And his cohorts were gleaming with silver and gold.

The iambic foot (short-long) of blank verse would have less of the gallop in it. One might say that, for lines of conflict,

> A remarkable help is the anapaest here;
> Paramount are its claims on the listening ear.

Now Paramount is chiefly known as a film-company's label. Whether all the pictures thus scheduled merit so proud a word I do not know. But, for once, an industry, which is usually barbaric in its use of language, chose and retained a word of strength, of tradition, and of musical quality.

PARAMOUR

THERE is the same anapaestic vigour in paramour as in paramount. I have commented before on the inadequacy of our lexicon of love. Paramour, however, has melody on its side and often is the making of a line. Marlowe knew the word to be paramount and used it to swell the diapason of his yearning Faustus:

> O thou art fairer than the evening air,
> Clad in the beauty of a thousand stars,
> Brighter art thou than flaming Jupiter,
> When he appeared to hapless Semele,
> More lovely than the monarch of the sky
> In wanton Arethusa's azured arms,
> And none but thou shalt be my paramour.

Spenser, too, had a taste for it:

> Bring hither the Pink and purple Columbine,
> With Gillyflowers:
> Bring Coronation, and Sops in wine,
> Worn of paramours.

One would expect the Old Testament to be full of paramours. Ezekiel's Aholibah, symbol of Jerusalem whose whoredoms he arraigned in the grand manner of a really peevish Major Prophet, 'had played the harlot in the land of Egypt, doting upon their paramours'. The translators of the Bible used paramour only this once and it is queer that they should have managed to get through the Song of Solomon without recourse to it. Shakespeare, too, employed it strangely little and you would think that having rolled it on his lips in Romeo's magnificent finale

> Shall I believe
> That unsubstantial Death is amorous,
> And that the lean abhorred monster keeps
> Thee here in dark to be his paramour?

he would have let fly with it again. Yet it is absent from the major tragedies and, just as the Biblical translators found no use for it in the Song, so Shakespeare steered his way through Antony and Cleopatra's Egypt without turning to this easy (and paramount) conclusion to a sounding line.

PARAPHERNALIA

THE word, so descriptive of a clutter of small objects, comes to us from Greek matrimonial law and custom. 'Pherne' is a dowry; 'para' means alongside and so can signify outside. So paraphernal property was that which a wife retained when the dowry or phernal goods had been handed over to the husband. Hence paraphernalia were the lady's personal bits and pieces. In England they have come to signify all kinds of odds and end, gadgets, and titivations. The descent has been one from property to 'props' – in the theatrical sense. Popularity ensued because of the word's good, long, rolling noise: it spills everything that is 'in the bag'.

Until a friend pointed it out to me, I had never stopped to think about this monstrous six-cylindered word for small things. And he, in his explanation of 'sesquipedalia paraphernalia' went astray, opining that 'pherne' was the bed and that paraphernal matters were the bedside books, clock, pills, potions, and other occupants of the bedside table. A nice derivation but, unfortunately, incorrect. The surplus-to-dowry explanation wins.

PHRENZY

WHY does frenzy seem so much more furious when spelled with a 'ph'? Is it just the power of antiquity and the unusual? I do not think that I would so much enjoy the idiocy of Thomas Rymer's famous dismissal of Shakespeare if he had wound up with a mere 'f'. The 'ph' contains such a syphonful of contempt.

> Shakespeare's genius lay for Comedy and Humour. In Tragedy he appears quite out of his Element; his Brains are turn'd, he raves and rambles, without any coherence, and spark of reason, or any rule to controul him, or set bounds to his Phrenzy.

Phrenzy is correct if we stand by our Greek, as we do in the now fashionable schizophrenia which means division of the mind, the mental aspect of a split personality. The origin lies in the Greek word *phren* meaning mind, and the adjective phrentick oddly meant going out of one's mind instead of staying in it. Phrenology is the scientific study of mental faculties, while phrenzy or frenzy is the reverse of any such thing. I once wondered whether Shakespeare meant quite as much by frenzy as we do when he talked of the poet's eye in a fine frenzy rolling. Might not that frenzy be more akin to rapture than to madness? But elsewhere he links frenzy with fits and seizures. In *King John* –

The Lady Constance in a frenzy died.

Phrenticke became our frantic and Shakespeare used the word of the lover immediately before attributing frenzy to the poet:

The lover, all as frantic,
Sees Helen's beauty in a brow of Egypt.

and he is matched with the lunatic who 'sees more devils than vast hell can hold'. Frenzy, so far from being phrenetic or intellectual, was usually a nervous tumult for Shakespeare. Yet it could be, at best, an extreme form of imaginative ecstasy, the rapture of a man possessed by beauty. It was for the former 'phrenzy' that the foolish Rymer faulted him, not understanding his possession by the latter.

PICKSOME

I NOTICED this word in a *Times* obituary of Holbrook Jackson, that keen student of the eighteen-nineties and of good book-production in all ages. To be a picksome man is not, I think, to be a pernickety man: the latter is a fuss-pot or possibly worse. The former is fastidious, and to be thus selective, thus picksome, is surely a virtue. Do we suggest a fault if we use the adjective fastidious? Surely not. Nowadays we have the slang word 'choosey' invading this range of meanings and the 'choosey' man is certainly regarded as being picksome to a tiresome extent. In this array of epithets for the precise and careful chooser the Scottish perjink is admirable. Finical and finikin are also useful and attractive adjectives, but they express a distaste for the too sedulous taster, which fastidious does not. I do not know who invented fuss-pot, but it gives a vivid impression of somebody boiling over with 'choosey-ness'. One hears the fuss-pot simmering with his whimsical addictions and dislikes. The picksome man, as I conceive him, is cool and works on judgment not on excitement. He ranks with the connoisseur and curioso, not with the finical tribe. A fashionable epithet of the time is hand-picked, to signify carefully chosen. It seems to me silly; especially when applied to candidates for jobs. These the wise employers selects not manually, but mentally, in a judiciously picksome way.

PING-PONG

I WAS reminded by some playful verses from Stewart Perowne of the fortunes of this word and sport.

My trusting teachers taught me
The lilt of lute and song;
A likely lad they thought me
But they, alas, were wrong;
I played ping-pong.

But teachers today would honour a Table Tennis international as one of the swiftest creatures alive, a prodigy of dart and dive, recovery and sudden smash. Expertness in ping-pong, if we can still call it so, can now get you a handsome income on the music-hall stage as well as some international sporting honours. The game seems well worth a place in the Olympic Games, which it does not yet receive, although the official laurels are lavishly bestowed on a wide range of athletic oddities. There is a case perhaps for leaving out croquet, that noble *al fresco* mixture of billiards, chess, and pleasant places, on the ground that its opportunities and appeal are limited, but is Table Tennis for ever to suffer Olympic disregard because it began life with a nursery name? Ping-pong was an exact 'according-to-noise-made' title and I have a friendly feeling towards it still: the word now appears to give the cold shudders to those who take this exercise in earnest. As a domestic pastime it becomes intolerable for adults, especially in a heavily furnished room, unless you have a slave to recover the ball that is pinged and ponged. Ping-pong has a far-eastern ring and it suitably came to us, I think, about the time of *San Toy*, *The Chinese Honeymoon* and other Oriental pleasures of the lighter stage.

POPPING-CREASE

THE vocabulary of England's game of cricket is, on the whole, unimpressive. Brevity, not splendour, is its merit. What simpler than bat and ball, in and out? Yet the latter couple have their complications for the stranger, as this extract from *The Natal Mercury* demonstrates. It is said to be an Englishman's definition of cricket to his American companion.

> Cricket is really quite simple. You have two sides – one out in the field, one in. Each man in the side that's in goes out in turn to have his innings, and when he's out he comes in (or out) and the next man goes in until he's out. Then, when all are out, that ends the innings, and the side that's out in the field comes in, and the side that's been in, goes out and tries to get those coming in, out. Sometimes, of course, you get men who are still in and not out. When both sides have been in and out including not outs, that ends the game.

The one term in cricket which has a kind of absurd glory is that which describes the line on or about which the batsman stands to play the ball just under four feet from the wicket. This is called the popping-crease, presumably because, if he gets outside it, somebody will pop the bails off his wicket and so put him out. Popping-crease may, of course, mean striking-line, i.e. the place where the batsman has a pop at the ball. That, I think, is the orthodox view, but I prefer the idea of his being popped out by the wicket-keeper.

Pavilion is a fine-sounding word, worthy of its place both on Cleopatra's barge and in *Hymns Ancient and Modern*. But it is not a monopoly of the cricketers. Popping-crease, however, is, and back from popping-crease to pavilion go the unskilful, the unlucky, or the merely injudicious.

POWDER

THIS in a letter from South Lancashire:

> During the war years my wife worked in the N.A.A.F.I., in a local camp. She found that a favourite word with 'other ranks' and their female opposite numbers was 'powder', and that it was used in the sense of going absent without leave. I find the word in the *Shorter Oxford English Dictionary* as follows:
>
> > Powder. V. collq. and dial. 1632. Intr. To rush; to hurry with rushing speed; said esp. of a rider.
>
> Here, apparently, is a genuine survival in Lancashire dialect of a seventeenth-century word, which has disappeared from 'educated' speech, with only a slight alteration in the meaning.

My correspondent goes on to quote Caldicott's 'Three Jovial Huntsmen' who 'powdered up and down a bit and had a rattling day'. I had associated this kind of powder with pother or pudder, i.e. banging about. If King Lear could call his storm 'a pudder o'er our heads', pudder was obviously a strong term. Nowadays powder has many domestic and personal applications. 'To powder one's nose' is polite feminine English for leave the room. So a powderer might be a quitter, which indeed was the Service usage described.

The same correspondent reminds me of the word Traundal. A traundal, who is to be found in Froissart, is obviously the very reverse of a powderer. Froissart, discussing the speed of Scottish invasions of England, said that the forces travelled twenty-four miles in a day and a night being 'all a horsebacke, without it be the traundals and laggers who follow after afoote'. Traundals have evaded the *O.E.D.* They may possibly be a mistake in writing for trauchals, since trauchle in Scots is to walk with dragging feet. Or there may be a link with our English trundle, to roll along or push. Those who have seen the Scottish tinklers slowly pushing their barrow-loads of just saleable junk along Highland roads, might well think of Froissart's traundals, following the horsemen 'afoote' and pushing up baggage in the role of camp-followers.

A trundler in my boyhood was a slow bowler at cricket. Is he still? He came into my vocabulary when I was writing cricket-reports for the School Magazine. It was a point of honour and of high regard in our journalese of those days never to use the ordinary word and always to seek out absurd similes and alternatives. We sought to outdo F. B. Wilson of the *Daily Mail*, who was then setting a keen pace in this kind of lingo. Bowlers, in our prose, did not bowl out batsmen: instead, trundlers beat the willow-wielder all ends up. Trundlers also sent down daisy-cutters (shooters) which turned out to be niggers in the wood-pile (i.e. upset the wicket), while a man caught at the wicket after some big hits was described as 'neatly pouched by the timber-watcher after harassing the rural areas with his cow-shots'. Footballs (Rugby) were spheres, ovals, leathers; and goals were uprights with horizontal attachments. Our Reports ran thus: 'After Boodle had raced round to score between the uprights, Foodle added the major points by placing the oval sweetly over the horizontal.' There was no paper shortage in those days.

The word powder would have come in usefully there. Boodle might have 'powdered through' to score, if he had gone at the gallop. On the other hand, if he had zigzagged his way, jinking the opposition, might he not be said now to have beetled his way through? A father who told his son that he had arranged for the boy to visit Norway received the following answer:

'Absolutely wizard, flash, whizz-o, grand, lovely to beetle up to Norway'. The adjectives oddly decline in vehemence of ecstasy, but the beginning is unbeatable and whizz-o, surpassing wizard, is new to me. I should have thought that to go swanning up to Norway might have been better than beetling. To beetle is a nice verb, whether applied to brows, cliffs or movement. Flash, as the equivalent of the old-world spiffing, stunning, smashing, in the vocabulary of juvenile gusto, is brief and vivid. But I am wandering, traundal-wise, far from the original subject. Indeed, like the Jovial Huntsmen, we have powdered up and down a bit.

PREVENT, once meaning come before, was an encouraging word, in complete contrast with the present significance. Asking the Lord 'to prevent us in all our doings' is certainly not an appeal for hampering or frustration; we leave that to our terrestrial rulers. Instead, it implies assistance. The old and new meanings of prevention seem to coalesce in William Collins's *Ode to Evening*:

> Or, if chill blustering winds, or driving rain,
> Prevent my willing feet, be mine the hut,
> That from the mountain's side,
> Views wilds, and swelling floods,
>
> And hamlets brown, and dim-discovered spires;
> And hears their simple bell, and marks o'er all
> Thy dewy fingers draw
> The gradual, dusky veil.

(What a fine adjective for spires! And I like the 'gradual, dusky veil'.)

Prevent here means both anticipate and dissuade. The arrival of bad weather comes too soon for one who is earlier demanding to 'rove some wild and heathy scene'.

How many words are there which now have two completely contradictory meanings? Prevent is one of them. Let is another. Church goers (C. of E.) on the 4th Sunday in Advent learn, after being let in to the Service, that they are 'sore let and hindered' in running the race that is set before them.

A correspondent sends me this from Newman's *Dream of Gerontius*:

> SOUL What lets me now from going to my Lord?
> ANGEL Thou are not let: but with extremest speed
> Art hurrying to the Just and Holy Judge.

I have already mentioned 'Presently', which still means 'immediately' in Scotland, whereas in England the word now generally signifies' later on'. Also I have dealt with secure and security, which until the eighteenth century meant careless and carelessness, involving danger, whereas Security Measures now mean the exact reverse.

Apparently is sometimes used to signify obviousness, more often likelihood.

Any others?

PROBE

HEAD-LINE English has forced probe into continual usage. Inquiry and examination are longer words and more cumbrous. Harassed sub-editors, when dressing 'copy', have to find captions that will run in a narrow column; they naturally delight in such brevities as probe. The smaller newspapers become, the more probes and fewer examinations and investigations shall we have. I have just seen an inquiry into a fatal explosion in a factory described as a Blast Probe. If monosyllables make good English, then sub-editors are masters of the linguistic art. They are probers to a man. School examinations, however, have long been reduced to exams; so we need not, as yet, read that a great public figure was noted in youth for failing in his Maths Probe.

It was an ingenious journalist who first applied this surgical term to public inquiries. Quiz is shorter by one letter and it must be remembered that, in designing captions, a single letter can make all the difference between fitting in and failing altogether. Thus, where MORALS PROBE might not be squeezed in, VICE QUIZ might very well do the trick and I have seen Vice Quiz for a Police Investigation into crime often enough, but rather more commonly in America than here. While on the subject of these brevities, it is worth noticing the enormous head-line popularity of the little word bid for attempt. Three letters! That is precious indeed. Were our British police headquarters to make an inquiry into an attempted murder we might, if the present vogue continues, read on top of the news YARD PROBES SLAY BID.

PYRAMID

I HAVE written before of Pyramid, as a fine soaring word in an iambic line, especially with the Greek plural in four syllables, as in Cleopatra's cry,

> Make
> The high pyramides my gibbet.

I have also dwelt on syllabubs as a sweet conclusion to the feast. But when I find pyramidal linked with syllabub I needs must quote. Here was Parson Woodforde's idea of an 'elegant' dinner:

> The first course was, part of a large Cod, a Chine of Mutton, some Soup, a Chicken Pye, Puddings and Roots, etc. Second course, Pidgeons and Asparagus. A Fillet of Veal with Mushrooms and high Sauce with it, rosted Sweetbreads, hot Lobster, Apricot Tart and in the Middle a Pyramid of Syllabubs and Jellies. We had Dessert of Fruit after Dinner, and Madeira, White Port and Red to drink as Wine.

After this he reports 'we were all very cheerful and merry'. What would happen to us now? Have we lost, in our hard times, all stomach for such a fight? The mere reading of such fare almost turns one queasy in these lean times. That hot lobster in the middle of it all! How much was it polite to miss? My impression is that most of the diners had a dip at quite a lot of it. Pyramidal times!

RACY

RACY means, in the first place, characteristic of the native. Charlotte Brontë wrote of Yorkshire families as being, 'racy, peculiar and vigorous'. Racy came to be used of all distinctive things, especially in relation to soil and locality. The ordinary reader, on first seeing the word, is apt to confuse it with racing and think of something swift. There is, indeed, some connection with the two kinds of race here, because fast can mean raffish as well as speedy. (Is this usage disappearing? Does anybody under sixty now speak disapprovingly of 'a fast girl'? The rates of this kind of motion have risen so sharply that the word seems a trifle tame. We have moved on to more vigorous dismissals.) 'Racy of the soil' is generally applied to language and conversation and by racy talk, I imagine, is meant something not altogether reputable, at least when the phrase is used by august and solemn persons.

I came across racy not long ago while turning out a drawer and discovering an ancient wine-merchant's catalogue. What a lingo the craft employed – and may, I hope, employ again, when at long last they have enough stock on their hands at a price possible for ordinary folk and so have to cry their wares as of old!

The vintners' English had a pleasing variety of words and of application of words. 'Full-bodied, stout, shows great breed.' This referred to a Clos de Vougeot, not to a Champion Clydesdale. 'Exhibits great finesse' was used of a white Bordeaux and not of a bridge player. 'Medium body, elegant, very ready' might fitly describe a house-maid or a motor-car. It did, in fact, describe a claret. 'Smooth, vinous, very high class' suggested to me an advertising agent. But it was the description of Château Cos d'Etournel, 1928, from the region of St. Estèphe. The words 'stylish and racy' brought to the mind's eye a perfectly brogued and tweeded beauty photographed at some Point-to-Point Steeplechases with shooting stick and leathery friend. They belonged, in fact, to a Rhein wine.

Wines are continually 'generous', like race-horses, and often 'animated', like conversation. I have seen wine described as spacious, and the author who used the adjective probably had the 'spacious days' in mind and thought to give his bottle a romantic quality. But surely 'spacious days' is one of the most idiotic descriptions of Elizabethan England, in which lack of space was the chief characteristic of all social life. The roads were narrow, town streets mere alleys, houses packed and close, windows small, roofs low, beams projecting and menacing, clothes swaddling, and ruffs smothering. Spacious, referring to our own epoch of vast and speedy flights and conquest over space, is certainly more sensible. But for Tudor times it has a grotesque falsity.

Nicely aromatic as wine catalogues may be, there is a case for improving them by bolder usage of the transferred adjective – that is to say, by applying to the liquor the qualities which it is expected to evoke in others. If I were in this line of authorship I should announce 'This ice-cutting, shell-opening, unbosoming sherry', 'This chatty and confident claret', 'This champagne of great wit and repartee', 'This courtly and consequential port, a wine to damn the Government and bless dessert', 'This raffish, anecdotal brandy', 'This sage and pensive whisky'. Yes, there will be room for new minds and fresh nibs in the wine-vaults.

Advertising in general ought to quicken our language. So many of the brightest young men from the University put in a year or two as copy-writers for an advertising agency and some of the most notable literary figures appear to be well settled in this craft, secretly writing up pills and patent goods by day in order to afford the luxury of composing at night the books which they really wish to write. Where a fresh touch is especially needed is in the real estate business. Are we to go on hearing eternally about 'wealth of old oak' and 'old-world gardens'? Is a small house to be for ever 'bijou', are the large houses always to be 'commodious' and 'to stand in their own grounds' (they would not be much good if they stood in somebody else's), and are the said grounds to be 'extensive', world without end?

There should be room for some of our liveliest epithets here, racy included. Why should not a Cotswold manor-house, beautifully fitting the hills where it grew 300 years ago, be called 'racy, full-bodied, showing great breed'? It happens to be simple truth. Is that always calamitous in salesmanship?

RATHER

HOW many people who use the word 'rather' realize that they are using the comparative form of the now antiquated but still beautiful adjective 'rathe', meaning quick or early? Milton's rathe primrose might have been called by him 'rather than the buds of May'. You can see the word's progress clearly in Lady Macbeth's cry,

We fail,
But screw your courage to the sticking-place
And we'll not fail. When Duncan is asleep
Whereto the rather shall his hard day's journey
Soundly invite him – his two chamberlains
Will I with wine and wassail so convince
That memory, the warden of the brain,
Shall be a fume and the receipt of reason
A limbeck only.

The usual pronunciation of rathe is with the 'a' long, as in rage, and the dictionaries support this. But how many actresses, playing Lady Macbeth, say 'rayther' when they come to this line? In accuracy, they should do so. But they would be thought nowadays to be practising some form of dialect – or affectation.

Just as sooner came to mean 'more willingly', so rather lost its temporal urgency for urgency of desire or purpose ('I'd rather be right than President'). The decline of this fine word to mean merely somewhat, as Damon Runyon might have said, is sad. 'Rather a pity' hardly sums it up.

SCROUNGE

MY note on scrump, which I thought meant steal, often applied to theft of apples, brought the reply that a scrump is in some places the apple itself. Farmhouse cider in South Devon is called 'scrumpy'. In that case to talk about 'scrumping apples' would be as unnecessary as to say 'fishing for fish'. No sooner had I read this answer than I was confronted by a statement in the *Listener* that 'scrounge seems to have originated from a dialect form 'scrumpe' or 'scronge' which means to steal, *especially to steal apples*'. It is odd how theft and apples go together in the public mind; perhaps not so odd if you cast your mind back to Eden. The note in the *Listener* continued:

No doubt the word was first used by schoolboys to mark a distinction between the activities of Autolycus and those of Bill Sykes. To pick up windfalls, even to climb trees and dislodge hesitating fruit, was not the sort of venial offence that ought to be termed plain 'stealing'; 'scrounging' is akin to poaching, therefore carries with it some faintly revolutionary flavour, as of poor peasants filling their bellies surreptitiously at the expense of the surplus possessions of rich squires. But 'scrounging' would hardly have risen to the dignity of a place in our national dictionaries but for the War. It then took on some of the functions of an older word, *foraging*. And so, by 1919, or 1920 (the authorities differ), 'scrounging' became diffused fairly generally through society by the returning warriors as a term meaning 'to hunt for, cadge, get by wheedling, or to acquire illicitly'.

Now the fashion has changed. First you fiddle (wangle) something, then you flog (sell) it. Fiddle and flog are by no means limited to apples.

A previous note on organize, snatched from the body ('the organized joints and azure veins') to serve the machine, especially the social mechanism, has brought me the reminder that it lately became a good Service word for scrounge. 'Let us organize a few cigarettes.' The village-boy will continue to scrump in the orchard; the barrow-boy in the town may organize the results.

SHIBBULDY

A CORRESPONDENT sent me this interesting, antique, and probably local word for correctly or properly. 'Do it shibbuldy', he was ordered by his father when given a boy's task. He offers two interpretations, either it was 'ship-buildy', i.e. trim, ship-shape, Bristol-fashion: or that it was a corruption of 'as it should be'. The localities said to use the term range from Cornwall to Oxfordshire. But if it is indeed a telescoping of 'as it should be' I smell Yorkshire in it and would like to link it with seesta (seeest thou?) 'Yon lad's alert, 'a does things shibbaldy, seesta?' Probably I am wrong, but that makes a pattern to me. Even with the ship-buildy derivation, Yorkshire still might be the source. Would they not do things shibbaldy in Whitby?

SKEW AND SKEWBALD

THIS survives chiefly in askew, but it is a good verb for swerving, jinking, shying, and even squinting. Eschew is another form of this avoidance. One thinks of 'eschewing evil' as a common piece of Biblical advice, but reference to Cruden informs me that the word is only used twice in the two Testaments. Odd how it sticks in the memory!

Is a skewer so called because it stops meat skewing? A curious form of *lucus a non lucendo*, if it is.

Skewbald is an attractive adjective belonging to the farm and the stables. Presumably a skewbald (more or less piebald) horse is so named because the markings of his coat swerve about and give an impression of baldness here and there. But W. W. Gibson distinguishes the two:

> Horses with manes and tails a-swing
> And spanking hoofs – cream, chestnut, bay,
> Roan, piebald, skewbald, sorrel, gray,
> Snow-white, jet-black. . . .

Presumably he limits piebald to black and white, with skewbald to suggest the other dapples.

SNUG

WHOEVER invented the word snug – the lexicographers can find no certain origin – had the right idea. It contains the very essence of a comfortable frowst. It suited the Victorians who were great wrappers-up and indifferent to the allure of an open window which now often works all too powerfully, some lovers of snuggery think, upon one's host or companions. Dickens, who had sufficiently learned about cold and hunger for himself in his boyhood, was a great addict of the word snug. While re-reading *The Pickwick Papers* recently I found myself continually be-snugged. Snug could be prosperous as well as cosy.

> 'And a very snug little business you have, no doubt,' said Mr. Winkle knowingly. 'Very,' said Bob Sawyer. 'So snug that at the end of a few years you might put all the profits in a wine-glass and cover them with a gooseberry leaf.'

Thackeray also dealt with folk 'lying snug', in wealth as well as in warmth. The famous phrase 'As snug as a bug in a rug' comes from Benjamin Franklin who applied it to a Mr. Skugg.

Snugs used to be regular features of well-conducted public-houses: they were usually small inner-rooms, frequented by 'the regulars' and almost reserved for them. They were dark, frowsty, and redolent of stale beer, tobacco, and decaying leather upholstery; they were the exact opposite of the chromium-plated, plucked-eyebrow style of hostelry now known as a Road-House. The snug, of course, had a coal fire and this ventilated the room a little. No decent frequenter would open the window of such a sanctuary. An early use of snug was as an adjective for neat and trim and I think that Shakespeare regarded Snug the joiner as a tidy rather than a cosy man. We know that he was 'slow of study' and that, cast as Lion, he roared but gently. I see him as a 'trig' little man and not as a frowsty, dishevelled patron of the snug.

SPIV

THE spiv, at the time of writing, is a masculine animal who lives by his wits without either working or breaking the law. Or at least he does not break the law so much as to be an easily arrested criminal. The windy side of it may be his habitat. His chief object in life, we are told, is to evade labour and thrive on deals of one kind or another. He favours a certain type of gents' suiting, with padded shoulders and a rakish cut. The toes of his shoes are as sharp as his wits.

There has been much discussion about the word 'spiv'. Some have assigned it to America, presumably on the ground that Britain lives on imports and that an American accent is now assumed to be necessary in all forms of light entertainment. Others have tried to explain it by its initials. If, in the official English of the Ministry of Education, Horsa means 'Huts Operation, Raising School Age', then surely Spiv, in colloquial English, must be Society for Prevention of Immoderate Virtue – or what you will. Or V.I.P.s (very important persons) in reverse. But all this is quite unnecessary. Spiv is a hardening of Spiff which meant two things to the Victorians. In one usage it was an adjective meaning smart, in another a noun meaning a salesman's commission or bonus. Obviously our spiv derives something from both the spiffs.

From the adjectival spiff came spiffy and spiffing. A spiffing time, for a fine time, has now an antique flavour and brings back to mind the masher who spooned. 'All spiffed out' was Gilbertian English for all dressed up. Spiflicate or Spifflicate, meaning confound or overwhelm, seems to be a different word altogether. It certainly does not mean smarten and was in use in the slang of the eighteenth century before spiffs had appeared to enjoy their spiffing time. As I write, the British Government, in its search for extra sources of labour, is wondering how to spifflicate spivery and get the 'wide' boys to work. Deep is a common synonym for clever; it is queer that its opposite, wide, should have replaced it in Spiv-English. 'Wide' may be a contraction of wide awake.

> Our governor's wide awake, he is: I'll never say nothin' agin him nor no man, but he knows what's o'clock, he does; uncommon. Thus Watkins Tottle in *Sketches by Boz*.

SPRAG

COULD a spiv be a sprag? Sprag, or in South West England, sprack, is a sharp little word for a sharp little fellow. The best known use of it is in Parson Sir Hugh Evan's comment on young William Page in *The Merry Wives of Windsor*. 'He is a good sprag-memory.' Sprag has the authority of Lamb and of Sir Walter Scott, but the latter was definitely quoting Sir Hugh in his use of it. Sprags are also pit-props and young fish. Sprack, for quick, lively, reminds me of the German *spritzig*, which used to be employed by the wine-merchants to describe certain of their Rhine and Mosel wines. *Spritzig* sums up certain types of ebullient young persons, sprag folk who are aware of that quality and do not conceal it. I should like a verb 'to sprag'; i.e. to be clever in public. The lad who sprags is not necessarily a Smart Alec, because that phrase – whence came it? – denies real cleverness. The Smart Alec is, to my mind, somebody assuming a cleverness that he has not got. A Sprag is a genuine quick-wit, who shows it.

STALL

NOWADAYS stalling nearly always refers to an engine. Or one may stall off a bore. But stalled, applied to depressed human beings, is a good old usage. 'You look stalled' is Yorkshire for 'You look dull, you look as though your brain had stopped'. We might make this use of stall more general. Frustrated has been, inevitably, overworked by our years of controls, rations, and prohibitions of all kinds. Indeed, whenever I contemplate a day's work or leisure nowadays, I feel stalled. Either there is no paper, no print, no binding for the performance of the one; or there is no transport and no victuals for the enjoyment of the latter. Yes, we are bored with discussing our everlasting frustration: why not have, 'Ee, ah'm fair stalled' instead?

STILLICIDE

'I STILL remember', wrote Robert Louis Stevenson, 'that Emphyteusis is not a disease nor stillicide a crime.' Both are terms of Roman law and concern the holding of land. Stillicide refers by derivation to the falling of drops. The regulation forbade the owner of land to build to the end of his plot and so let the roof-water or eaves-drip fall on his neighbour's property. Stillicide proclaimed the necessity for a protective gap. It is not a word which many will have much occasion to use now, but it brings us up against the curious extension of meaning acquired by eaves-drop. When that word is spoken nobody thinks of eaves, but only of long noses and all too busy ears. Coleridge could still use eave-drops aright.

> . . . Whether the eave-drops fall
> Heard only in the trances of the blast,
> Or if the secret ministry of frost
> Shall hang them up in silent icicles
> Quietly shining to the quiet moon. . . .

The suggestion of standing under the eaves to listen has lasted for three and a half centuries and now it predominates altogether. If you said to your neighbour today that you had a complaint to make about his eaves-dropping, his mind would not turn to stillicide; rather would he angrily deny that he ever fell to practices so low. Stillicide remains as formidable as a Roman pillar, but its meaning is very much duller than its aspect. The look of it suggests assassination by poisoned alcohol or, as our murder-mongers would doubtless entitle a yarn thereon, 'Death in the Distillery'.

STRUMBLE

NUMBER Sixty, the last of Hilaire Belloc's epigrams in Rhyme (*Sonnets and Verse*, p. 180) has this (from the Latin) concerning humility:

Blessed is he that has come to the
  heart of the world and is humble.
He shall stand alone, and beneath
His feet are implacable fate, and panic at
  night, and the strumble
Of the hungry river of death.

Is strumble an invention? If so, we should be grateful. For here is the strong tumble of waters.

Strumble sounds Scottish to me. The glorious Tummel used to be a strumble indeed. (I know not what the electrical engineers have left of it now.) Douglas Young employs the vivid word whummle (overthrow, whirl away) to much the same purpose. In his beautiful memorial 'For Alasdair', a Scottish scholar, he writes of burning Africa from the side of a native burn, where the fisherman-poet stands, to cast his flies from a moss-covered stone.

The fowk about Inverness and Auld Aberdeen
aye likeit ye weel, for a wyce and a bonny man.
Ye were gleg at the Greekan o't, and unco keen
at gowf and the lave. Nou deid i the Libyan sand.
  The spate rins drumlie and broun,
  whummlan aathing doun.

Strummal or Strummel has (or had) several meanings in Scotland, but they are not Belloc's. Strum is not only to play coarsely on a musical instrument, but a pettish, sullen humour. A strummel (according to Jamieson) was a strumble or a person so feeble that he had to stumble. It was also the remainder of tobacco in the bowl of the pipe. Belloc's 'strumble of the hungry river of death' is a roar of dark waters indeed.

SURQUEDRY

SIR WALTER SCOTT knew surquedry when he saw it. It is an old corruption of the Latin *supercogitare*, to think too much, especially of oneself. I came across it, meaning arrogance, in Sir Thomas Urquhart's plea for a union incorporating Scotland with England.

> This was not heeded in ancient times by reason of the surquedry of the old English, who looked on the Scots with a malignant eye; and the profound policie of the French, in casting, for their own ends, the spirit of division betwixt the two nations to widen the breach.

It has since been supposed, by at least some English, that the Scots are the more surquedrous nation of the two. At any rate quite a number of Scots are now viewing the increasing domination of their land by London-made laws and London officials as a strong sign of surquedry on the English side of the Border.

TAMARISK

WE have sheltered our sea-side gardens and esplanades with this feathery, but firm-footed, importation from the East. Sheila Kaye-Smith well called a marine resort 'Tamarisk Town'. It is to me a strangely fascinating word. Also it is a happy word with happy associations. The holiday feeling and memories of sand-boy days whisper in its slender, scale-like leafage. Nobody writes better of these things than John Betjeman, especially when he remembers Cornish summers.

> O healthy bodies, bursting into 'teens
> And bursting out of last year's summer clothes.

In the evening light the very shrubs become fantastic, tamarisk not least.

> Now drains the colour from the convolvulus,
> The windows of Trenain are flashing fire,
> Black sways the tamarisk against the West,
> And bathing things are taken in from sills.

One child still zig-zags homewards up the lane,
Cold on bare feet he feels the dew-wet sand.
Behind him, from a walk along the cliff
Come pater and the mater and the dogs.
Four macracapras hide the tennis club. . . .

Macracapras are unknown, even to the omniscient *O.E.D.* But I like the sound of these wind-breaks for the players. Betjeman has a charming quality of mixing City and Surbuban with the Muse. His nursery and bungaloid themes seem to run naturally into iambics and I find no clash in such a collocation as this:

The lane, the links, the beach, the cliffs are bare;
The neighbourhood is dressing for a dance
And lamps are being lit in bungalows.

O! thymy time of evening: clover scent
And feathery tamarisk round the churchyard wall
And shrivelled sea-pinks and this foreshore pale
With silver sand. . . .

Tamarisk there again! A gracious presence. Were Betjeman ordered to write a sonnet to his bathing-suit or even to his first dinner-jacket, it would drive as deep into the heart as ever went boyish plunger into the blue water of a Western cove.

Kipling's 'Christmas in India' has tamarisks at the head of every stanza.

Dim dawn behind the tamarisks – the sky is saffron-yellow

leads on by way of high noon and grey dusk to

Black night behind the tamarisks – the owls begin their chorus.

It is a rather bitter chant of exile. But the tamarisks, brandishing their slender plumes over each verse, give it peculiar beauty.

TAMASHA

TAMASHA is an Oriental word defined as 'walking about for recreation or amusement'. Later the walking part of it was forgotten and tamasha settled down in Victorian English of the Anglo-Indian type to signify 'fun and games'. What I like about the original tamasha was its linking of the walk with the enjoyment. We have a fair number of words for walk or stroll: we may perambulate, saunter, daunder, dander and so on. Generally a dander is a pleasant form of exercise. But it is not necessarily so and a man might saunter or dander with no song in his heart but only curses on his lips. Pessimists and misanthropes can stroll with every manifestation of spleen. But a tamasha is a joy-walk and is forbidden to be the exercise of the afflicted. None the less it does somewhat resemble the Christian name of a young lady in a Chekhov play, such a one as dreams of Moscow nights and murmurs the immortal Chekhov line, 'Since the tea isn't ready, let's philosophize a bit'.

Your true tamashist would only philosophize after tea when his whole being was soothed with the beneficent action of that 'water bewitched'. The best kind of tamasha surely occurs in the late afternoon when winter is fading out and life is springing up, when to feel the new length of light and the influence of the too-long-forgotten sun adds richly to the ordinary pleasure of a dander. In towns the lights come out as the offices empty and pink slashes the dove-grey of the sunset sky: people are trotting off home or hovering happily on the brink of plays and pictures, with a beat of the heart and a light in the eye, tamashers in both senses. In the country the evening mist lightly floats upon the coppice and there is a glint of the fairest of all our greens, that of the larch in spring. That is the true hour of tamasha, rural species.

TASSEL-GENTLE

I SUPPOSE that myriads of school-children, ploughing, before their proper time and unaware of its verbal miracles, through

Romeo and Juliet, have written informative notes about tassel-gentle, the male peregrine falcon.

> O, for a falconer's voice
> To lure this tassel-gentle back again.

What a suave word it is for so formidable a bird of prey? The sport of hawking, which has long ceased to appeal to more than a handful of the relics of the landed gentry, was obviously well-known to Shakespeare. Bate for quiver (of wings) is a common word of his and I have elsewhere traced 'batting an eyelid' to that kind of bate. We find the falconer's bate again and also his hood in Juliet's imagery. What a sporting household that of the Capulets must have been! Hawks and hoods swoop through its lingo. Juliet calls thus on 'civil night':

> Hood my unmann'd blood, bating in my cheeks,
> With thy black mantle.

Tassel-gentles, when unhooded, bate their wings in the void, then stoop to the lure, and this use of stoop for swoop is not only Elizabethan. It lived on in poetry and was well used by Swinburne:

> We are not sure of sorrow
> And joy was never sure;
> To-day will die to-morrow,
> Time stoops to no man's lure.

But would Swinburne have known a tassel-gentle had he seen one, as he well might? The peregrine still occasionally visits London and stoops to the lure of a fat, soft, urban pigeon.

TERSE

TERSE means something wiped, therefore clean, spare, free from extra weight or length. We are reminded of this because of our present recourse to 'detergents', which is officialese for soap substitutes. When a newly appointed Bishop entered his Palace he found it so unpalatial as not to contain a single bar of soap. Having applied to the appropriate authority he was informed:

'It is much to be regretted that saponacious material cannot be found in the Palace, but we would suggest that other detergents may be available.'

In view of this masterpiece of verbose, evasive officialese, it seems odd that detergent should have any connection with terse.

THREAP

OF the many English words which now survive mainly (perhaps only) in dialect, 'threap' is a good example. It is a most expressive term for constant asseveration. 'I keep threaping at them' nicely – or sadly – sums up the miseries of the form-filling citizen who is trying to get an answer out of the authorities. To threap is cited in the *Translations of the Yorkshire Dialect Society* (Vol. VII) as East Yorkshire for 'to maintain by persistent assertion', but threap was certainly no dialect rarity in Elizabeth's reign. Sometimes it meant rebuke. One could threap down on the ignorant or contumacious: more generally it referred to repetitious argument or statement. The child with a grievance threaps away: so does the club bore or the senior resident of the sea-side and holiday hotel. Whether or no one loves the Government of the day, there is a limit to listening to the threapers against it. Why should the East Riding of Yorkshire keep this short and satisfying word to itself any longer? England has need of it.

THRIBBLE

A NICE word for making do and muddling through. I came across it in a passage by Richard Brome, one of Shakespeare's successors. He introduces into his play a nobleman, who is organizing a play. He seems to reply to Hamlet's speech to the player and to justify 'gagging'. The nobleman says,

My actors
Are all in readiness, and I think all perfect
But one, that never will be perfect in a thing
He studies: yet he makes such shift extempore,
(Knowing the purpose that he is to speak to)
That he moves mirth in me above the rest,
For I am none of those Poetic Furies
That threats the actor's life, in a whole play
That adds a syllable or takes away.
If he can thribble through and make delight
In others, I am pleased.

An accommodating nobleman certainly, but what the author of the play thought of this thribbling is another matter.

I cannot discover whether thribble was a particularly theatrical word or whether it was of general use. If it was theatrical, the players are foolish to have lost it. It is curious how many stage-terms survive from Shakespeare's time and have never, presumably been out of use. The prompter prompted for Burbage as for Sir Laurence Olivier. Benvolio in *Romeo and Juliet* talks of the 'without-book prologue, faintly spoke after the prompter'. The book, i.e. the script of the play, was even then the book. Parts were studied, until the actor was perfect or word-perfect as happens now. Webster's Flamineo in *The White Devil* has a magnificent farewell to the life which he has used so ill. 'I go', he says, 'to study a long silence.' The surprise of silence, instead of part, is superb. If thribble was commonly employed then, the more folly to let it go, for it is a most expressive term, with its suggestion of an improvised dribbling of the lines. We have most of us seen some wretched actor, caught short of his words, thribbling faultily and showing his distress. Perhaps Brome's kindly nobleman would have pardoned even that – provided the fellow showed some invention.

TINTAMARRE

WHAT became a galimatias and later, via France, a brouhaha, was, in the seventeenth century, a tintamarre, which sounds French too. But lexicography leaves its source unidentified. Tintamarre, used by Evelyn and Vanbrugh among others, was a clatter; workmen in the house annoyed the former with the tintamarre of their instruments. It was also a clatter of voices: the modern cocktail party, with its close pressure, tinkle (or crash) of glasses, and strident babble of voices, is a tintamarre-factory. The Scottish usage of clash for gossip, creating the goodly word clashmaclaver, carries on the idea of clatter as well of chatter, but it is more usually applied to idle prattle than to mere din. Our habit of living in ever smaller and less soundly built premises, together with the ubiquity of broadcasting, continually adds to the tintamarrish quality of life. This is no period in which to lose such a word – or indeed any term which strongly or amusingly signifies assault upon the ear-drums.

TOYT

THIS from Yorkshire: 'You must find this word-taking a very interesting toyt. I think toyt comes from toy or is somehow connected with it.' My friend adds that such good old English as 'Not I, marry' is still naturally used in his locality, although I suppose very few who now use this form of affirmation realize that they are calling on the Virgin Mary. The same letter tells me that the word 'Spurring' is used for putting up the banns at church. 'Have you been spurred?' 'Marry, I', would mean 'Have you had the banns up?' 'Certainly.' Spurrings he connects with the Scottish speiring, which means asking. In that case it would be one of many terms which linger in the Pennine Range: these mountains bestride the national Border and run more or less continuously from Derbyshire well into central Scotland with the same type of wealth, sheep above and minerals below, and the same type of native, shepherds and miners. Naturally, although the accent alters continually from dale to dale, and country to country, a certain number of dialect words remain common to both, and the word-lover may indulge his toyt very happily in Cumberland and Northumberland where Scots and Pennine English mix their vocabularies.

TREAKLE

I LIKE treakle for a sticky kind of trickle. This from Suffolk – an old woman speaking: 'I axed passon, Passon do ye give me a pew under your pulpit. There's Mrs. Robinson and Mrs. Smith sit right afront of me, and by time your sarmon treakle through them two, that do sound wonnerful poor stuff, that there really do.' We have all heard speeches – don't let us put all the blame on the clergy – that treakled through the audience in just the same way.

TWACH AND OTHERS

THAT excellent poet, Lord Herbert of Cherbury, wrote of a twaching kiss in a poem so complete in its survey of osculation that it must be amply quoted,

Come higher Womankind and all their worth,
Give me thy kisses as I call them forth.
Give me the billing-kiss, that of the dove,
    A kiss of love;
The melting-kiss, a kiss that doth consume
    To a perfume;
The extract-kiss, of every sweet a part,
    A kiss of art;
The kiss which ever stirs some new delight,
    A kiss of might;
The twaching smacking kiss, and when you cease
    A kiss of peace;

The music-kiss, crotchet and quaver time,
The kiss of rhyme;
The kiss of eloquence, which doth belong
Unto the tongue;
The kiss of all the sciences in one,
So 'tis enough.

Quite enough kisses. But not, perhaps, enough of Lord Herbert's hand and fancy.

Even the larger Oxford Dictionary knows nothing of twach, a verb which must be left to speak (or kiss) for itself. But I am grateful for being driven to the Twa's, since there I find Twatchel, an earthworm, Twattle, meaning chatter, and Twattle-basket for chatterbox. Now that basket has become a shunt-word for bastard in English slang and popular humour the term Twattle-basket dismisses a prattling bore with even greater vigour. This leads on to the mystery of twerp, who was a human twatchel. I say 'was' because twerps have recently appeared to be on their way out, as the saying goes. The date of the twerp's flourishing was about 1930, I think. Prune, for duffer, replaced one aspect of twerpery, but there was something of meanness in a twerp which is not included in the prune.

VAPOURS

DOES nobody ever have the vapours now? Are all our young ladies for ever vapour-free? Few maladies have had so beautiful a name. Vapours were supposed to be exhalations of the organs rising to affect the brain and to agitate the nervous system. Crudely put, wind. Well, wind round the heart sounds poetical enough, but such vapours can mean agony of the most material kind. Falstaff attributed 'crudy vapours' to the brain, vapours to be dispelled by the wise through plentiful addiction to sherris-sack. One knows that 'crudy vapour' feeling, even if the rather sickly potion suggested strikes one as a far from proper remedy. We would rather prescribe a more astringent carminative to suit the sharper palate of a spirit-drinking age. Falstaff might have enjoyed better health on whisky and soda than on sherris-sack.

Vapours, of the climatic kind, have a more melancholy charm than mere mist. I disagree with Hamlet's naming of the globe as a 'pestilent congregation of vapours'. The word is too good for such world-dismissive talk. Pestilent congregation of fogs, certainly. But vapours, no. Tennyson knew better:

> The woods decay, the woods decay and fall,
> The vapours weep their burthen to the ground.

That is essential autumn. And of course the Bible translators saw the value of its sound. 'For what is your life? It is even a vapour that appeareth for a little time and then vanisheth away.' The alliteration, with the interlacing of v's and a's, is masterly.

I like vapouring, too, for idle, fantastic talk. Celia Fiennes, that undaunted traveller of the William and Mary roads of England (or what passed for roads) wrote of a fellow-traveller who 'drew his sword and vapoured' when some imagined peril was at hand. She meant that he blustered, or perhaps only twittered, not that he swooned. Nowadays politicians often talk of one who gets up and 'waffles'. Waffle has only dictionary status as a batter-cake to be eaten hot with butter or molasses. It is a good invention for empty talk, but not, I think, as sharply descriptive as the old word, vapouring.

VERILY

I HAVE been asked to make a plea for the return to ordinary speech of Verily. Certainly it is a more musical word than truly. In repetition 'Verily, verily' makes a beautiful double-dactyl for the student of classical scansion and of its values in English speech. I suppose that Biblical associations now bear hardly upon the fate of words; to be linked with Parson and Sunday School, with Second Lessons and clerical intonations, causes words to be discarded amid the tacit anti-clericalism of our times. Since verily was so much and so fully used in our Authorised Version, I looked up a Shakespearean Concordance to see what place it had in the poet's mind and usage. The result was surprising. Shakespeare used verily ten times in all in his plays and five of these instances occur in one of the plays. Which? *The Winter's Tale*. Why? Had he been listening to a preacher who dealt in 'verily's'? He might then have been impressed by the quality and music of the word with the result that it sprang up from his subconscious mind with uncommon frequency just while he was at large among the rages of Leontes and the revels of a shepherds' feast. It is possible.

There is a warm and pleasing roll of the 'r' in verily, which gives even to so cumbrous a term as verisimilitude a special kind of attraction. Verity is one of the best of the 'virtue' names for girls and comes more sweetly on the tongue than Patience and Prudence, though both the latter have, verily, a grave beauty of their own.

VERMIN

THE case of vermin raises the interesting question whether the meaning of a word can affect the value of its sound. Association of ideas must, I suppose, break in: but it is against all logic that a word should be deemed ugly because of the nasty thing to which it is applied. Most of the unpleasant articles have, as a matter of fact, titles unpleasing to the ear. No charm of sound is attached to dung, offal, sewer, smell, stench, stink, sweat, and so forth. But the issue was raised in the case of vermin. Robert Hichens, in his autobiography, recalls this conversion with Sir Max Beerbohm. (It was Max's habit to call Hichens 'Crotchet'.)

> One day he said to me, 'Do you think, Crotchet, a word can be beautiful, just one word?'
>
> 'Yes,' I said, 'I can think of several words that seem to me beautiful.'
>
> 'Ah?'

A pause.

'Then tell me, do you think the word "ermine" is a beautiful word?'

'Yes,' I said, 'I like the sound of it very much.'

'Ah?'

Another pause.

'And do you think "vermin" is a beautiful word?'

The answer, as I see and hear it, is that vermin is quite an attractive, if not a beautiful, word. Its origin among worms, its transference to 'rats and mice and such small deer', does not alter the fact that it is, in sound, close neighbour to the rich vermeil and vermilion: both these ride well upon a poet's line. Supposing vermin had a loftier, even leonine, significance and we met such a verse as,

Where mighty vermin of the forest roar,

should we dismiss it as contemptible? Ermine (Erminea Mustela) is a name for the unpleasant stoat. As the Max-Crotchet conversation suggests, it comes well off the tongue as well as looking well in places of ceremonial assembly. And vermin takes the ear no less.

VILLA

VILLA has lived a life of sad declension. Originally and Romanly, it was a country mansion, complete with home farm. For hundreds of years it remained in rural life to signify the finest thing in housing. In Italy, and through Italy's influence, it lived on through the Middle Ages with magnificence. A Palladian villa might be a masterpiece of design and considerable in scale of luxury. The 'Villas and Cabinets of Noblemen' saved the word from slur, at least until the middle of the eighteenth century.

Then two forces worked the ruin of villa. One was the new desire for rustication so vividly described by Cowper. This new suburbanism had its snobbery and that was the second enemy of the villa whose name it greedily annexed. 'The mechanic at his dusty villa' (Dr. Johnson) is typical of the decline and fall of the once proud and imposing label. Here is Cowper's picture of the semi-rural brick-box masquerading as a villa –

> Suburban villas, highway-side retreats,
> That dread the encroachment of our growing streets,
> Tight boxes neatly sashed, and in a blaze
> With all a July sun's collected rays,
> Delight the citizen, who gasping there,
> Breathes clouds of dust, and calls it country air ...
> There prisoned in a parlour snug and small,
> Like bottled wasps upon a southern wall,
> The man of business and his friends compressed
> Forget their labours and yet find no rest. ...

This is a fair description, I fear, of much contemporary living and sums up the cabin'd life of the 'quiet week-end' in an 'old-world' cottage (all beams, stairs, draughts, and no room to sit down). The bungaloid retreat is perfectly hit off by Cowper's sarcasm at the expense of toilsome leisure.

O.E.D. first discovers the contemptuous term 'villadom' in 1880. I like the rare verb 'villafy', almost punning on vilify, to signify cheapen or spoil a site with villas. From time to time some classically-minded citizen endeavours to restore the dignity of villa and rescue it from the associations of a dull gentility. James Agate, for example, when he was the occupant of a house near Swiss Cottage, named it with a Renaissance flourish, Villa Volpone. Villa has been hardly treated and deserves such a chivalrous and rescuing hand.

WALKABLE

NOBODY can explain why amorous means loving and odious not hating but hated or meriting hate. Once more it is just the perversity of English usage that is at work to the mystification of the foreign student. In the same way the adjectives ending in 'able' show curious variations of meaning. I am tired of sizable, now so much in vogue for well-sized. The active use of the termination 'able' I once discovered in the nice phrase 'barkable dog'; but usually 'able' is passive. An admirable man is not an admirer. But what of a 'walkable child'? The epithet, I am reminded, was used by G. C. Coulton in his autobiography, *Four Score Years.*

> For about two years, while Edmund was in the nursery and Beatrice still unborn, I was the youngest walkable child.

Walkable here seems to me to move or sway delightfully between the active and the passive. A walkable footpath is purely passive: a walkable man purely active. But a small child, in the first efforts towards an upright motion, is both independent and assisted. He or she walks, but is also supported or pushed in the great adventure. So walkable in this case is surely a perfect adjective. Upward and onward with the nursery walkables!

WINGEY AND OTHERS

GRUMBLING, whining. But not dictionary English. Wingey may be a concertina-word, whining and cringing being run together. For the same thing a Newcastle correspondent sends me 'pittering'. Pittering has an orthodox dictionary meaning. To pitter is 'to make a rapid repetition of a sound in quality approaching the short "i", as in the thin sound made by the grass-hopper or by a thin stream of water running over stones.'

Do cascades pitter in the blaze of noon? Does the fell-side beck pitter instead of plash when stricken by a summer drought? Perhaps. But I think the pittering child, at the end of a long day in the sun, all passion for the play and the feasting spent, is the better usage. Wingey brings to me, because of its likeness to cringe, an element of fear. The pittering child suggests a fractious kind of fatigue, intensified by a sensation of vomiting to come.

Scots and Irish naturally keep the 'h'. Their children are whingey. A whingey child who gives his toy a swingeing blow would give it a dinge or dent. This kind of dinge presumably is cousin to ding for strike or beat. I like the Scottish on-ding for the violent drive of rain upon a windy day. In the soaking streets of some grey town, even more than on the moors, it is easy to be whingey at such an on-ding as that. There is no pittering about an on-ding.

YARD

I MENTION this word not because of any intrinsic beauty but because of the queer usage which it receives in newspaper headlines. What would a foreigner, who thinks he has mastered English, make of this banner-caption in the paper that he buys on landing? BRIGHTON BODY MYSTERY: YARD STEPS. Is some Brightonian, he might ask, walking in paces three feet long? If so, what is the mystery? Does not every adult walk with some such pace? Or is there a perambulant corpse? The Englishman, on the other hand, knows that Yard means (in headlines) Scotland Yard and Scotland Yard means the Criminal Investigation Department, where the chief hunters of crime are gathered together. Hence Yard Steps are police moves of the high-up kind.

Our evening papers dote on Yard. 'Yard Man Calls.' Blessed brevity! With the narrowing of the column in order to squeeze more into the dwarfish papers of wartime and after, the problems of the sub-editor, endeavouring to put as much information as is possible into a headline, become more teasing than ever. There always had been great need for monosyllables. Something could be borrowed from the American Press, e.g. the use of slay for murder, (American language being, as usual, more Biblical and old-world than current English). Inquiries, questions, investigations were rendered impossible by length: hence their replacement by quiz and probe, on which I have already made some comment. Yard Probe manages to say quite a lot in nine letters about a police investigation to an English reader, but what a puzzling suggestion of a long, sharp instrument it would give to the stranger!

Most of the commonly used long words are forced out of captions and so handier alternatives have to be found. Parliament becomes Lords or Commons, with M.P.s always available. Attempt always becomes bid. WIFE SHOT IN HELP BID, I have just read, a most graphic chain of monosyllables.

Where a long name can hardly be altered, initials may help. The liner *Queen Elizabeth* becomes Q.E. because Queen Bess would be misleading. With Southampton long ago reduced, in football reports, to So'ton, Q.E. DOCKS AT SO'TON becomes manageable 'captionese'. For similar reasons politicians are esteemed for the brevity of their names. (Chamberlain was a handicap, Cripps is an asset to the owner.) Educational legislation becomes Schools Bill, and Oxford and Cambridge are headline BLUES instead of Universities.

After coping with Yard Steps and Yard Probes, the foreigner must then accustom himself to the mysteries of Cricket and other sporting 'banners'. He must learn not to tremble in a Test Match summer at ENGLAND IN PERIL. Nor must he swoon on reading that ENGLAND COLLAPSES. The more concentrated type of Stock Exchange information will also be a mystery. If he reads KAFFIRS BOIL UP he may think that cannibalistic murder is afoot and that Yard Steps are badly needed in return. He can hardly know that only a rise in gold shares is being implied.

YESTER

THERE is a veil of sadness over that letter 'y'. Yearning is a more melancholy word than longing. Youth? It is not a comfortable word on the ear and goes best with the backward glance of those who regret advancing years. Youth Movements sound to me incurably grey. What of yellow? Rather ugly, as the colour, too, can be. Yield to the yoke? Drab terms of surrender. Year is essentially a sad word and fits perfectly into regretful reminiscence. 'Take from seventy years a score.' Days more often go with happiness, though of course they have also been woeful enough and have led to bloody sunsets. What a noble shout of happiness is in Belloc's 'Dedicatory Ode':

And oh! the days, the days, the days,
  When all the four were off together:
The infinite deep of summer haze,
  The roaring boast of autumn weather!

Suppose he had written, 'The years, the years, the years', the happiness would have seemed less. And then come those evocations of the Cotswold scene where the river-names ripple like the rivers themselves:

The quiet evening kept her tryst:
  Beneath an open sky we rode,
And passed into a wandering mist
  Along the perfect Evenlode.

The tender Evenlode that makes
  Her meadows hush to hear the sound
Of waters mingling in the brakes,
  And binds my heart to English ground.

A lovely river, all alone,
  She lingers in the hills and holds
A hundred little towns of stone,
  Forgotten in the western wolds.

It is only when the sombre thought breaks into this magnificent poem that years occur:

But something dwindles, oh! my peers,
  And something cheats the heart and passes,
And Tom that meant to shake the years
  Has come to merely rattling glasses.

I surmise that, when poets are in a wailing mood, the word year bubbles up from the subconscious: when they are happy, other periods spring to their lips. Hours are often glad or laughing. Weeks, for me, have no quality at all.

Yesterday is a longer word than need be. Yester was enough at one time. Then, I think, the usage of yesternight, yestreen, and yester-year (what phrase more mournful than 'the snows of yester-year'?), made it customary to add day also to yester. So we gained this word of lamentation, for ever lighting fools 'the way to dusty death'. All the poetry of the glass-in-the-hand and sob-in-the-heart order rings with yesterdays. Fitzgerald's 'Omar' continually sounds the bell:

> Ah, fill the Cup: – what boots it to repeat
> How Time is slipping underneath our Feet;
> Unborn Tomorrow and dead Yesterday
> Why fret about them if Today be sweet?

Kipling used it for monitory purposes:

> Lo, all our pomp of yesterday
> Is one with Nineveh and Tyre.

His lines strike deeper than of old. Few pomps belong to Britain now. 'O call back yesterday, bid time return' is the everlasting music of regret and much assisted by the sadness of the initial 'y'. I began this book with some observations on the plaintive quality of a long 'a', as in alien; I end with that letter trailing its doleful beauty through dead yesterdays in company with the penultimate letter of the alphabet, also a mourner.